Pinch Me

BETH ROWLES SCOTT

To Mildred —

Pinch Me

A LONG WALK FROM THE PRAIRIES

— for great days in Surrey!

Beth

GRANVILLE ISLAND
PUBLISHING

Library and Archives Canada Cataloguing in Publication

Scott, Beth Rowles, 1928-
    Pinch me : a long walk from the Prairies / Beth Rowles Scott.

Includes index.
ISBN 978-1-894694-74-2

    1. Scott, Beth Rowles, 1928-. 2. Women teachers—British
Columbia—Surrey—Biography. 3. Teachers—British
Columbia—Surrey—Biography. 4. Surrey (B.C.)—Biography.
5. Education—Kenya. 6. African Canadian Continuing
Education Society. I. Title.

LA2325.R68A3 2009   371.1'00820971133   C2009-903543-X

Artist: Lyn Noble
Editor: Renate Preuss
Text and cover design: Nadja Penaluna
Indexer: bookmark: editing & indexing

The bridge and raft shown on the cover were built by Thomas Rowles,
the author's father, on Moose Jaw Creek, Saskatchewan.

All photos were taken by or are in the collection of Beth Rowles Scott and
her family with the exception of the photo of Mercy in Shitaho School
taken by Jay Procktor, www.jprocktor.com, the photo of Francis Butichi
taken by Karen Jensen, and the photo of Beth and pupil in Kenya (page
213) by James Haga.

Granville Island Publishing
212–1656 Duranleau
Vancouver, BC V6H 3S4
www.granvilleislandpublishing.com

First published September 2009 • Printed in Canada

This book is dedicated to the
memory of Mother and Father,
Lydia and Thomas Rowles.

Acknowledgements

When I began to write *Pinch Me* I declared that I most certainly did not want to produce a memoir: I enjoyed the writing process and would see where it might take me. With such lack of direction where *could* it take me? To frustration. To a cry for help.

So I sent some of my words to Jerrold Mundis, a professional writer and writer's coach. Jerrold told me immediately that, whether I liked it or not, I was writing a memoir. Well. From that time forward his advice was invaluable to me. I enjoyed working with him.

Why not ask my friends for their assistance? Indeed, they did help me: Gwen Murray spent hours spotting silly errors in the text; Donna VanSant and Morag MacKendrick encouraged me throughout.

As I had known they would be, my sisters, Jeanne and Dorothy Rowles, were keen to read recollections of our early years. They were my champions. Dorothy offered forthright criticism — just what I needed. Cousins Ted Douglas and Fred Chapman also readily helped with memories and photos.

It was an unexpected bonus to meet Mary Ellen Reid during this writing project. She was generous with her insights and knowledge.

It has been a pleasure to work with Jo Blackmore of Granville Island Publishing and the people she called on to put *Pinch Me* together: Nadja Penaluna, designer; Lyn Noble, artist; and Renate Preuss, editor. Talented professionals, all.

But most of all, I am grateful to my dear husband, George. He never withheld his criticism and never wavered in his support. As always, he was my *olwanda*, my rock.

Contents

PART THREE Late Blooming

Introduction

Pinch Me. Why pinch me? So I can be sure that this happiness I feel is not a dream, that my life has really changed so much since I was a fat little girl in Saskatchewan.

Growing up, losing my fatness and leaving my home province was sometimes fun, sometimes painful, often challenging. But what about this happiness? Did I really find it? Should I have expected to? There were times when I would experience happiness, but then I would lose it again. When I caught a glimpse of it, it had a habit of slipping out of sight. Happiness seemed to play games with me. Does it play hide-and-seek with everyone? Surely there is a way to grab happiness and keep it.

I never did find a way to trap it. But I did have enough sightings of this elusive, mysterious happiness, and enough help from those who loved me, to give me a formula from which to make my own happiness. I tested the happiness formula again and again and eventually believed that the findings were true enough to be released, here, to the public.

This story presents happiness as it was found by that once fat little girl from Saskatchewan, Beth Rowles.

Perhaps you have found your own way to happiness. But if you have not, do taste the ingredients of the *Pinch Me* happiness brew. May they serve you well!

Until one is committed there is hesitancy, a chance to draw back, always ineffectiveness.

Concerning all acts of initiative (and creation) there is one elementary truth, the ignorance of which kills countless ideas and splendid plans:

That the moment one definitely commits oneself, then providence moves too.

All sorts of things occur to help one that would never otherwise have occurred.

A whole stream of events issues from the decision, raising in one's favour all manner of unforeseen incidents and feelings and material assistance, which no man could have dreamt would have come his way.

Whatever you do, or dream you can, begin it.

Boldness has genius, power and magic in it.

Attributed to Johann Wolfgang von Goethe
(1749–1832)

PART ONE

PRAIRIE ROOTS

The Prairie Lily is the provincial floral emblem
of Saskatchewan. Whenever Father spotted this
orange flower, he seemed to claim it as his own.
Its bright blaze of colour lit gloomy days
with a ray of hope.

The Coats

The Coats arrived in a very large Eaton's box that Father brought home in the wagon. He had picked up the box at the post office in Moose Jaw. Even though he had left the farm before daylight, it was after dark when he got home, for the journey to Moose Jaw was a full seven miles and the wagon was powered by a team of draft horses. They plodded along steadily, without complaint, but they were not speedy. Father had followed a carefully crafted route that included the grocery store, the hardware shop, the post office and the library. Neglecting to pick up any necessary item would be a disaster, since at least a month would elapse before there would be another such odyssey. We did have a car, mind you — a 1928 Star, still shiny and new looking — but it was up on blocks, lolling in the yard because there was not money enough to buy gas to keep it on the road. The Coats, therefore, were brought home in the wagon.

A large Eaton's box was a fairly common sight in Saskatchewan in those days. The leading department store of the day was the T. Eaton Company established in Toronto in 1869. Its first mail-order catalogue appeared a few years later.

The mail-order service that Eaton's provided helped to alleviate the isolation that was endemic amongst the settlers on the Prairies. The catalogue itself was an important furnishing in Western Canadian homes; indeed, farmers called it "The Homesteader's Bible." Milking machines, wedding dresses, sets of dishes — even my grandparents' house — were purchased by means of an Eaton's catalogue order. What's more, for years young children learned about the anatomy of the opposite sex by turning to the selection of underwear displayed in that book. When outdated by the arrival of the next edition, the Eaton's catalogue found its way to the outhouse where it came to an end, so to speak.

The Coats had been ordered through the catalogue several weeks before and so we knew very well what the big box contained. It had to be opened carefully. (We didn't cut string; we untied every knot, for string was precious and was wound onto the string ball that was kept in the cupboard along with pencil stubs and the dregs of a bottle of glue.) With my two sisters, I pushed in close, eyes round in anticipation.

The Coats were monstrous. They looked awful. Could these be the same garments that we had seen in the catalogue's fall edition, where they had looked soft and lovely? These things were neither soft nor lovely. They were made from some kind of fabric that had a deep pile with bristly cut ends, stiff and rather hard so that when you ran your hands over the fabric, it felt a bit like patting a dog — but not one you wanted to pat again.

When I modeled my Coat, I felt even worse. I did not look at all like the pretty girl in the Eaton's catalogue. She was tall and slim and her hair was long and blonde and hung down in ringlets. Pretty girl in pretty coat. I was not tall. And I was fat. My dark brown hair was cut square — straight across the front in fairly short bangs, straight down the sides to the middle of the ears and then straight across the back. Square girl in square coat.

The worst part of all was having to pretend that it was all just fine. Sending The Coats back was not an option, nor was complaining.

It was 1935.

Pretty Lady

I have asked myself: Who was my role model? Who would that have been? Try as I may, I cannot think of any particular person upon whom I aspired to pattern myself. Was the lack of a role model a large deficit in my development? Maybe not. Maybe there wasn't one particular idol, but several of them: a number of people, each of whom possessed a certain idol piece that I greatly admired and wanted to emulate. The various characteristics — such as appearance, scholarship, commitment — might not have appeared together in one single icon, but individually in a number of them. In sum, I did have a role model.

If so, then the first part of that composite that I recall was the appearance role model. She was the prettiest lady I had ever seen and I saw her only once — at the Moose Jaw Fair when I was seven years old.

We attended the Moose Jaw Fair because Father had entered three cattle in the dairy farm division. He believed that these three — Sadie, Bessie and Sophie — came close to meeting a number of criteria established for the Holstein cow competition. Father thought they had the right roundness of belly, size of udder, straightness of spine and glossiness of hide to be eligible for special notice. These worthies were transported to the city with the same team of horses and in the same wagon that had been used to collect the Coats. (Dairy cows wouldn't walk the seven or so miles to the fair, so they were actually in the wagon.) They were deposited beside a large low barn and assigned to a particular stall. Father stayed all night with them — an excess of devotion, it seemed to me, but absolutely necessary, for the cattle had to be fed, watered, milked and groomed. Father watched over them as if they were gold-plated. And although they were not judged to be winners, they made a good showing in this rather large country exhibition.

My sisters and I were thrilled to be taken to the fair. I was quite in awe of all the farm entries, from the multi-coloured Bantam chickens to the huge prize-winning bull anchored in a stall not far from the one occupied by our three well-manicured cows. The bull swung his great head — as big as our round kitchen bathing tub — until he loosened the rope that tied him in his stall. As his handlers scrambled to regain control of the bull, Mother and we three girls reduced ourselves to two-dimensional cardboard-like figures, pasted against our end of the barn. Father stood very still. The bull's keepers managed to attach a long, thick stick to the ring in the animal's nose and thereby cowed him. ("Cowed" may be a poor choice of word here.)

Where did Father sleep, I wondered. "Well, just there in that manger," I was told. I had never imagined any real person sleeping in a manger, although of course I knew that Jesus did.

We soon left the barns to tour the midway. Well! What a revelation that was: the tallest man, the fattest woman, the two-headed dog, clowns and balloons everywhere. We just gawked and gawked. We weren't much for rides and thrills. I suppose we went on the merry-go-round, although I don't remember that we did. We were all pretty timid and Mother was cautious, keeping us under her wing like the chickens we were. To our amazement, she bought tickets for us to go inside a tent to see a dance show. We sidled in through an entrance flap and scurried straight along over the sawdust floor, between rough board benches to the very front of the tent where we sat on the foremost bench right before the raised platform.

Almost as soon as we sat down, loud music accosted us, filling the tent with unexpected sound that stunned us a little. Then there was a great fanfare and from the sides of the stage eight beautiful ladies glided onto the platform. How lovely they looked — powdered faces, lacquered hair, long, slim legs and high, high heels, their bodies hidden behind great feather fans that they moved gently while swaying to the music.

It was like a dream. These visions floated one at a time to either side of the stage until there were two ranks of legs, fans and heads. Then, down through the centre of the eight minced one more doll right to the front of the platform and right in front of our goggling eyes. I had never seen such a pretty lady — blonde, slim, beguiling. So pretty. All that I might ever hope to become.

To my utter dismay, Mother suddenly gathered us together and, like a partridge scuttling her chicks under a bush, she bundled us out through a crack below the edge of the tent. She didn't tell us why we had to leave like that, just that we couldn't stay any longer. Why was there laughter from men in the audience as we made our exit? It wasn't until some years later that we teased Mother about her naivety in taking us to a "girlie show," where she had unexpectedly glimpsed nakedness behind those waving fans and had realized that the pretty ladies were dancing for quite a different clientele than we three small farm girls.

I wonder if I ever told her that one of those small farm girls had found a dream that day. A role model. Her beauty icon.

Caron

"Magritchy raised the rent." At least that's the way I heard it. What happened was that Mr. MacRitchie, the owner of the farm we rented near Moose Jaw, told Father that the price of the lease would be increasing before the year was out. I suppose that people said we were forced off the land, but however it was, our parents had to find another place to live and to make a living. We had rented the Moose Jaw farm for five years, from 1932 to 1937.

Mother and Father had been early victims of the Great Depression. They had invested their savings in a farm near Swift Current, and had lost it all after every crop in the next three years had failed. By 1932 they were relegated to the status of renters. The Moose Jaw farm that they found to lease, what I knew as the Magritchy place, was pretty and right along Moose Jaw Creek. To leave it must have been another tough blow during those desperate years.

They found another place, though, in a neighbourhood called Caron, not more than thirty miles away. Here was a farm for rent that even looked like a better bet than the Magritchy place had been.

But the Caron place was scary right off the bat.

To start with, moving the cattle to the new farm was a monumental task that had to be accomplished carefully. After all, our fifteen cows were the source of our livelihood, for Father sold the milk they produced to the dairy in Moose Jaw. This marketing would still happen from the Caron farm, so getting the beasts there safely was all-important. It was not so simple. At one point, Father had returned to the Magritchy place to bring the last of the cattle when the ones that were already at the Caron farm got out of the barn and started to bolt. Mother was very brave, running to close one gate while we three girls stood guard at another one. I guess she was more frightened than us because we didn't really understand what was happening — that the cattle had decided to try to go back to the old familiar farm. Mother got them into the barn and settled down before Father returned with the last of the lot.

The large house could have figured in a gothic novel. The cavernous downstairs rooms, almost empty with our few bits of furniture, echoed our footsteps and our voices. Upstairs an impressive number of bedsteads and mattresses had been left behind, replete with bed bugs. Lye soap fixed that problem, of course. A great attic was accessed by means of a forbiddingly steep set of steps, and at the very top of the house a captain's gallery provided the finishing touch.

As scary as it looked, for me the big old house was a fun place. But the school was awful. Too bad about that, for the nearness of the school — only a mile away — was one factor that had encouraged our parents to rent this farm. The Magritchy place was three and a half miles from the school, too great a distance for us in the winter months. Mother, a trained teacher, had helped us to learn at home.

My younger sister, Dorothy, was barely six, so she had never been to a school; I was supposed to be in second grade, although we didn't stick to established levels; Jeanne was nine and two years ahead of me. I hardly remember the few months I was in school when we lived on the Moose Jaw farm, but I have a very terrible memory of that school at Caron. I was absolutely terrified of Miss York, the teacher. Every Sunday evening I would have a stomach ache — which even then I didn't believe was real and I don't think my mother did either. Eventually, though, she took me to see the doctor, who found that I had a bladder infection. To this day I know that there had been nothing wrong with me at first, but somehow my body had taken pity on me and created an infection. It kept me out of school for a few days.

Grandfather Rowles' farm, 1930

After my brief "illness," I could think of no further escape. One morning I threw something of a tantrum on the way to school, lying down on the ground in the middle of the path. My sisters were kind to me — just waited until I came to my senses and followed them along the trail. It was probably that very day that Miss York went after the tiniest boy in the school. (There were only ten of us.) She picked him up, held him to her shoulder height and shook him. At lunch time, I went home.

The next morning, Mother walked with us to the school and spoke to Miss York. After that, things seemed to go along quite smoothly all day. When it came time to go home, Miss York came over to me and said, "Now you don't think you can get away with that kind of behaviour, do you, young lady? You missed two hours of school by leaving the way you did, and so to make up the time you will stay for half an hour each day for four days."

Funny the way that incident seemed to be a sort of catharsis for me. I don't remember being terrified anymore. I suppose I thought that if this was the worst she would do to me, I could handle it. But more than that, my family never condemned me; indeed, they seemed to want to protect me. The matter was never discussed. I was left with the feeling that, if there was folly here, it was *our* folly, not just mine.

At about the time that I finished my penance, we moved away from Caron almost as suddenly as we had arrived. On our last day, Miss York put her face right up close to mine and said, "Do you know what I think of you, young lady? I think you are a sissy."

Ever since those few weeks at Caron and my little tantrum, I have thought that there is a bit of madness in me. But I know I am not a sissy.

Green as Grass

Before I was eight, I had not known what a lawn was. A farmer's daughter, especially one growing up in the Great Depression, thought that whatever land you were lucky enough to own or rent was meant to be devoted to agriculture, to the business of making a living. To think of growing grass just for it to be looked at, to be mowed to a level surface, to be watered to keep it green, was quite a preposterous idea. To think that our family would live where we were surrounded by acres of lawns was equally surreal, but that is what happened when we moved to the Forestry Farm.

Because he had a bachelor of science degree in agriculture, Father had been able to get an appointment as foreman of the Forest Nursery Station near Saskatoon, usually called the Forestry Farm. This job was much below his level of experience and ability, but it was made attractive by a veiled promise that it would lead to him becoming superintendent of the farm within two or three years. Besides, this move gave our family the prospect of much greater security than there had been at either of the farms, at Moose Jaw or at Caron. Father had applied for this job before we left the Moose Jaw farm, but the letter of acceptance was much delayed and had not arrived until after the move to Caron. Now suddenly, the bad times seemed to be veering off a bit: the request for release from the rental farm agreement at Caron was generously granted and the assured government employment was at hand.

The Forest Nursery Station was a federal government initiative that offered assistance to Saskatchewan farmers to help them counter some of the soil erosion that was destroying so much farmland. It produced seedlings for hedgerows for the farmers to plant as windbreaks between their fields. Caragana plants were the favourites; drought-resistant, they grow rapidly when young to form shrubs that can live for fifty years. At the nursery, seasonal workers bundled the seedlings together in the springtime and mailed them to the farmers who had requested them.

In the summertime, the Forestry Farm provided a park for the people of Saskatoon. The great sweeping lawns curved elegantly around copses of trees and were edged with well-tended annual flowerbeds. No "keep off" signs deterred visitors from setting up a picnic on the grass, and hundreds of people enjoyed the lawns and flowers on Sundays and holidays. But on other days, this green, grassy idyll was our playground. We lived in a park.

It was not only the grass that was green. My family and I were green as grass in the business of city-like living. So much was new to us — running water, electricity, bathtubs and flush toilets. Imagine how it felt to be able to bathe in a huge tub of hot water when we had been bathing all of our lives in a basin, or to have a bright reading light after knowing only coal oil lights during the long winter evenings. We were country mice who had come to live in the city. We made mistakes, like plugging the toilet with unacceptable waste or forgetting to draw the blinds for privacy on Sundays, when strangers from the city would picnic on the lawns in front of our house. For the most part, we had arrived in a little bit of heaven.

Socially we were green, too, or at least I was. I was eight when we arrived at the Forestry Farm and sixteen when we left. I was not comfortable with others until I was at least fifteen years old. I do remember that there were girls who offered friendship to me, but I was not comfortable enough with them to provide my part of a friendship. I always felt different. I *was* different: I was fat and I had funny clothes.

Living at the Forestry Farm did not help with the socializing. We were not in a country community and we were too far from Saskatoon to be in the city community. We didn't have much chance to interact with others because of our distance from school; we always needed to hurry to catch a ride from school, to go straight home. I was socially retarded. It was a greenness that didn't buff off quickly.

I loved the praise that followed upon good marks, both at home and at school. It helped me put up with being fat. However, in grade nine, one of the boys mowed down that particular greenness: he told me that the only thing I cared about was getting the best marks in the class. I learned to be very quiet about the good grades, at least at school. People were surprised that I finished grade twelve at the top of the class.

I did have one very awful learning problem: I couldn't get over the horse, the one in the gym. Every time I tried to leave the springboard and leap over that ugly thing, I just froze. How I hated the physical education classes when we practiced gymnastics! I never did find out why I couldn't vault over the horse, but my failure to do so was probably a major reason for branding myself an athletic moron. I had my revenge ultimately, though. Not only did I buy and love riding a horse — a real live one of my own — but eventually I came to be head of the physical education department for a very large school district.

With Father's new job, we could at last afford dental care. Mother's teeth were in bad shape and so were Father's. Mother just had all of her upper teeth pulled. Tragic. Stoic, too. Father was able to maintain some of his — enough to get by, except for appearance. The dentist fashioned a partial upper plate that corrected his looks; the dentures were never comfortable, so not worn during his foreman labour days, but they were always necessary for greeting visitors or for city forays. He could easily forget to wear them. We'd be on our way to the city and hear, "Tom, your teeth. Tom! Your teeth!" Sometimes we had to go back for them. That wasn't funny. Jeanne would look worried, I would want to giggle and Dorothy would withdraw.

Some city relatives lived near us when we moved to the Forestry Farm: Father's Uncle Tom and his family. Great Uncle Tom's children were already grown and each of them had become a great success — three had PhDs, one had married a doctor (just about as good) and one, the best one of all, was full of fun. The only one who had stayed at home was one of the PhDs, Edith. She not only had her doctorate, she was a paragon of virtue. Edith might have been my intellectual role model if I had not been blinded by thinking that she was the epitome of spinsterhood, a state to be avoided at any cost. Much later I realized what a lovely lady she was.

Sometimes we were invited to have Sunday dinner at Great Uncle Tom's house. I think he and his wife, Trudy, and his daughter, Edith, were consciously trying to take some of the country out of us. The table, for instance, was always beautifully set with lovely china and sparkling silver. And there was the matter of the Sunday roast. Having been a butcher before he came to Canada, Great Uncle Tom knew how to carve the joint ceremoniously, standing at his end of the table, saying, "Very nice, my dear Trudy," then sharpening the shining knife on the steel. As he sliced off the end of the joint, we would behold *rare* meat! What a sight! (Our meat was always cooked grey.) Our eyes would dart around from one to another and Mother would suppress a grin. It certainly didn't bother me to eat some of the beast even though I felt like a carnivore; I gobbled away in my usual fashion.

No doubt Great Uncle Tom and his family helped to burnish our social graces and to do some city modeling for us. There was other modeling, too. I found some girls at school that I could emulate with a view to improving my persona. I let my naturally wavy hair hang down my back a bit instead of trying to tie it up to look like a movie star. I also copied the girls who did not turn down their socks but let them climb up past their ankles. (I only had one pair of socks that would perform in that way, so I washed them each night and wore the same ones every day.) And I practised smiling in front of the mirror so that I would not extend my mouth all the way across my face and up to my ears, the way it had looked in a recent photograph. Altogether, I thought I began to look less like a loser.

We lived amongst the green grass for eight years. These seemed to be the transition years — the years when I caught up on my retarded social skills, the years when I stopped being fat, the years when I found out that I could get good marks but that I had better be subversive about it, the years when I gradually didn't feel so ugly.

The Fat Factor

The fat factor loomed large in my early life. Is being a fat child such a terrible thing? Indeed it is. Fat children are at risk — physically, psychologically and socially.

I was not overweight when I was born, but by the time I was six I was a fat little girl. I don't think I was ever obese, but Mother was. Once, after she had consulted a doctor about a sore knee, she told me, "When the doctor stepped out of the examining room, I was so curious about my chart that I turned it around on his desk and looked at it. I saw the word 'obese' and turned the file right back away from me." Mother laughed about that, and for the most part she laughed about being fat. I didn't.

It was easy enough to succumb to fatness if you were a farm girl in Saskatchewan. The food was fat and starchy: lots of creamy milk, high-grade beef seamed with fat, and during the long winters only starchy root vegetables and no fresh fruit except for the mandarin oranges at Christmastime. The cooking too was heavily weight-producing with homemade bread, thickly sliced and plastered with butter; gravy accompanying all kinds of meat and fowl; potatoes whipped with butter and cream; puddings laden with sugary sauces. This kind of food was necessary to fuel men who expended a great deal of energy working on the farm; it was a menace for a young girl.

Lack of physical exercise was another contributor. I did not move around very much; I read books. Was lack of exercise one of the causes or one of the results of being fat? Was I physically inept because I was fat or was I fat because I was often immobile? Synergy, probably. In any case, when I reached puberty at about age eleven, I was sure I was very ugly and I knew where my biggest obstacle to beauty lay — in my fat body. I had not forgotten my appearance model — the beautiful lady behind the fan at the Moose Jaw Fair, slim and beguiling. I asked myself, "Do I have to be fat?"

Luckily I did not find it difficult to stop eating fatty things. I discovered what food made me fat and I just stopped eating it. I stopped eating porridge, claiming it made me sick, and I ate only half the sandwiches my mother made for my lunch. I lost my taste for potatoes and gravy, or so I said, and I decided that I didn't really like sweet things. After about a year of this, my aunts and uncles would comment, "Oh, my. How Beth has failed!" Failed? Bah. I was very deliberately, even stealthily, discarding my ugly fat.

Not only did I become thin, but I came to realize that I had some personal power. By taking control of the amount and the kinds of food I ate, I achieved a goal that I had set for myself. I was in charge. Recognizing personal power was a huge, unanticipated bonus that came with losing weight. It was a major victory in my teen years.

Losing weight and recognizing my personal power was, however, not all that needed to be achieved in order to overcome the legacy of the fat girl image. There was a significant deficit in feelings of self worth. I felt an affinity for Dickens' fat boy in *The Pickwick Papers*. This is what I read:

> There was the fat boy, perfectly motionless, with his large circular eyes staring into the arbour, but without the slightest expression on his face that the most expert physiognomist could have referred to astonishment, curiosity, or any other known passion that agitates the human breast ...

I noticed that Dickens didn't even give the fat boy a name. He was not graced with individuality or "... astonishment, curiosity, or any other known passion that agitates the human breast...." All he was remembered for was the invisibility that incidentally made him a great spy. I wanted to be more than a spy, more than an observer and auditor of life. I had to shake invisibility. I had to try harder to excel in those things that I could do well, and then be noticed and praised.

Mother had a precious "box" camera, but films for taking pictures were as impossibly costly as gasoline to run the car and so I cannot find many photos of myself taken during my childhood and youth. The few photos that I can find do not show an obese child; although I'm sure I was overweight, my self-image as a fat little girl was no doubt somewhat exaggerated. But I felt fat. That's what counted. Growing up in that persona was hurtful and left marks that took much more time than a year to erase. For a long time I could feel the scars blaze red whenever I was under a spotlight.

Play

As long as I can remember I've had trouble with the concept of "play." My first memory of the word was when Mother told us to "go out and play." She wanted us to get out from under her feet, to go and amuse ourselves, to find our own diversions. I think we disappointed her. For myself, I don't think I had much of the sense of fantasy that would have pleased her. For instance, the Moose Jaw farm was located beside a lovely little creek edged with willows, poplars and cottonwood — a setting that would work well for imaginary play, so Mother said. She would take us to a spot beside the creek that looked intriguing to her eyes and she would make some suggestions about how we could "play house," set up a door here and a bed there. Why would we do that, I wondered. We had a real house with a door and a bed. Why should we pretend? Mother would have brought some mending to do so that she could stay nearby. It just didn't seem to work. I would try to please her, but I really didn't want to "play house."

I didn't want to play with dolls either. One Christmas both Mother and Father went to lots of trouble to get me a very pretty baby doll and a cradle for it. They had gone Christmas shopping in Moose Jaw, a great occasion where, with much forethought, they purchased one present for each of us and one box of mandarin oranges for the family. At a bargain table, Mother had bought a doll whose eyes had come unstuck and were rattling around in its head. Doll parts were fashioned then from some kind of cardboard-like china, the parts assembled cleverly by fitting legs, arms and head onto the body by holes and knobs. At home Mother twisted the china head off the china body, glued the eyes in place and twisted the head back onto the body. Then she sewed a silk-like bonnet and cape for the naked baby, sacrificing a worn-out nightgown she had bought for her honeymoon. Father created a cradle for the pseudo infant using last year's mandarin orange crate. It was a lovely, thoughtful gift, treasured for many years. I just didn't want to play with it.

I did enjoy the houses I made from cardboard, paper and glue. Nobody thought the furniture that I produced was wonderful and I'm sure I don't know why I thought it was, except that it was my own idea. That may sound as if I was assertive, which I was not. But perhaps I was creative.

Although I was never one for much imaginative play, I know that Mother encouraged the development of fantasy and imagination in the three of us; she made sure of that part of our education. Because she was our teacher for months at a time when we couldn't get to school, she relied upon library books to enrich our schooling. She loved to read to us. The stories I remember most of all were written by Thornton Burgess. Familiarity with his little animal characters — Chatterer, the red squirrel; Sammy, the arrogant and handsome jay; Reddy, the sneaky and lethal fox — became part of our family culture. Beautifully illustrated, the Burgess books would encourage us to watch for birds and animals that we could identify, having met them in the stories. I did find some anomalies: for instance, Burgess describing the sun "disappearing behind the purple hills" seemed very odd to me because there were no hills on this flat, flat prairie, and purple was a garish colour in my crayon box. But Mother, perhaps remembering her own childhood in Ontario, read the words with such sweetness that they went unchallenged.

Mother also provided my first encounter with Peter Pan by reading J.M. Barrie's *Peter and Wendy* to us. It seemed to be a sad story, no doubt because it had been given to us by a lady who had lost her only child to diphtheria and Mother always seemed a bit low-key as she read it aloud. It didn't help that we left the precious book outside one night and the pages, even the cover, looked dejected ever after.

This education "at Mother's knee" initiated my love of books and the constant reading that was the best of play.

At school, games were supposed to be fun, but they were not very rewarding for a physically challenged fat girl. I remember a rubber ball that I really liked and that I played with endlessly at school and at home. One time a teasing boy at school grabbed it and threw it at the school, right through the open window of the principal's office. I braved this scary man's sanctuary and asked for my ball. He looked at me very sternly and said, "It's right here in my pocket and that's where it's staying." He did give it back to me, though, when I explained the situation (without tattling on anyone, of course).

We also played a game with marbles (agates) at home, but never at school with other children. If you won the game at school, by tossing your marble closer to the target than anyone else's, you kept all of the other marbles. Our parents considered the game played in this way to be gambling. We didn't get a very satisfactory answer when we asked how it was that all of the other kids at school could do this and we couldn't when it was so evil. Similarly, when we told Mother and Father about all of the swearing at school, they just said that we knew very well that it was wrong to swear and that was that. Coming from small, small country schools to this large city school required us, and our parents, to make some adjustments to our attitude and our behaviour.

A different kind of play was introduced to us by a charming elderly widow who gave each of us a ball of yarn and a crochet hook. That was the beginning of a lifelong enjoyment of handiwork; my pleasure was the kind of play that produced something. Knitting and crocheting were not usual pastimes for young girls. Such handiwork was a bit of a throwback to a former era, but it has stood me in good stead at times when I have been isolated or have for some reason faced idle hours or been bedridden or hospitalized.

My lack of playfulness was probably part nature and part nurture. In the first place, I was a passive, blobbish child; in the second, it is also fair to say that I was in a family that was not encouraged to hoot and holler. When I was about twelve, our cousin Ted Douglas came to live with us for some months so that he could get to school in the city.

The Rowles sisters: (l–r) Beth, Dorothy, Jeanne

He added buckets of hoot and holler to our whole family. Mother's nature seemed to change from sombre to sunny and Father sat less often, ruminating in his chair by the fire. Life was brighter for a while. Even when he left our home, some of Ted's aura of fun and his penchant for laughing at mischance seemed to remain with us. He was a great temporary brother who gladdened our lives for a while.

We did play board games, most often just one of us with Mother or Father, and most often on a Sunday afternoon. When we were growing up, we were not allowed to do our school homework on Sundays. I'm sure this discipline was more a tradition than a moral imperative: our parents did not work on Sundays, so neither should we. Anyway, our family's favourite board game was Chinese checkers. This game involved moving marbles from small holes to other small holes. Not very exciting. Other games, like Pick-Up-Sticks, would distract us too, but none were as durable as Chinese checkers. We lived in a land of long, cold winters with no television and no other families close by. Our family became closely bonded.

We were not encouraged to hoot and holler, as I've said, but we did occasionally become boisterous. Mother would always say, "You'll be crying in a minute." And so it seemed. Disaster struck me more often than my sisters. Excitement would get away on me until I would become a bit maniacal. An incident in point was a great floor-polishing game to shine the just-waxed linoleum floor in the kitchen, with the three of us running, leaping and sliding on pieces of a towel. I slid right into a window and shattered it — a catastrophe. Why couldn't I have been cut enough to require attention and sympathy rather than tolerance? Lucky to get tolerance, I'm sure, for replacing that window was costly and difficult. Another time, in high summer, we were playing with a tire, rolling it around the yard. I got very enthusiastic, pushed it too hard and away it went. Unstoppable, it rolled and bounced on and on, up over the fence and down into the creek. It floated happily along until it was right out of sight so that even Father was unable to reach it. It was an ancient tire, hardly worth keeping, but I thought I had lost a jewel. Father consoled me, "Stop crying, Elizabeth." (He called me Elizabeth when he felt special affection for me.) "You could not have guessed that it would leap away like that." I felt as if I were in the arms of Jesus.

Merriment was not big in my childhood and youth, but considering the times — the Depression and the war years — I wonder that we did not grow up with bitterness and harshness. That, we did not.

Prairie Winter

Christmas cards and calendar photos sparkle with images of glorious Canadian winters: skaters wafting along the river ice, country roads ribbonning through snowy fields, Aurora Borealis surreal in the midnight sky, festive sleighs coupled to frosty horses. If you lived on the prairie, you experienced all of these and you added your own winter stories of the coldest days, the deepest snow, the thickest ice. I have mine.

When my sisters and I were six to ten years old and it was holiday time, Mother would try her best to get us out of the house for at least part of each day. "Go out and play" just wouldn't work, though. We had to play very hard at something or freeze to death — something like learning to skate. We had some old skates: not three pairs for the three of us, but two pairs that we could pass around. Mother insisted that we could make a skating rink. She told us to push the snow aside from part of the yard so that the snow would make ridges that would hold the water for the ice. We submitted, albeit with a certain lack of grace, managing to clear the snow from a space a little bigger than a good-sized blanket. Then we got a hose and connected it to a faucet — not so easy, but she helped us. The task was to spew the water onto the cleared space. Some of the water escaped under the snow ridges and some of it blew back on us. The hose would never cooperate. The water froze in great lumps on our small rink, and the more water we added the rougher the surface became. We never did manage to get a smooth sheet of ice. "Just get your skates on and see what you can do," challenged Mother. *She* wasn't giving up. Tripping, crashing, ankle spraining, cold, cold — with any luck, the snow would start again and there would be a reprieve. Mother let us know that she was disgusted with our sloth and hurt because her daughters had no guts (not her word). Her uncharacteristic sarcasm hit home when she spat out, "Come on in, then, where it's nice and warm and you can read your books all day long."

At school we had been taught that we must have fresh air in our bedrooms at night, so we opened our windows just a tiny little crack. It's a wonder we could get the windows open at all because throughout the winter there would be a thick coat of ice on the inside of the panes. When Father saw what we were doing, he was very annoyed. "Shut those windows and leave them closed. I'm not going to heat all of Saskatchewan," he said, with unusual forcefulness. We muttered a bit amongst ourselves about Father not caring if we lacked oxygen, but we kept the windows closed after that.

Certain body parts were particularly vulnerable to the cold: noses and ears, of course, and fingers and toes. The velvety insides of the thighs would also freeze easily. Thick mittens, heavy socks and a good wool scarf were the solutions to avoid frostbite on the protrusions. As for the thighs, they were protected with the snow pants that we always wore on the coldest days. These pants were thick, heavy woollen garments that were worn to school either under or over the skirt. If you wore them under your skirt, you looked like a sack, especially if you were short and fat; if you tucked your skirt inside, it looked like a rag when you took off the pants. It had to be one way or the other because girls just never wore pants in the schoolroom. Once we were old enough to be in secondary school, we preferred the bruised feeling of the frostbitten thighs to the ignominy of wearing the snow pants. We had to hold strongly to our position on this: Mother thought that if we didn't wear the horrid pants we might become ill or barren.

For the little children in the city school, the teaching hours were truncated because the teacher needed time to prepare them for the short walk home in the cold. Not one was picked up by a parent, for in those days parents were not terrified that a crazy stranger would capture their children. It was the responsibility of the teacher, therefore, to make sure that all of the little tykes had their jackets properly zipped up, their toques pulled down over their ears, their scarves tied (that was very important) and their boots on the right feet. Preparing thirty-five six- and seven-year-olds to venture outdoors took more than a few minutes.

One little fellow who strayed from the group one day went over to the metal soccer goalpost and tried to taste the frost on it. There would not have been much harm if he had taken his tongue off the post quickly, but he didn't. His tongue stuck fast. The janitor who was close by took a mouthful of water from the fountain and spit it over the captive's tongue, which was immediately released by the post. The poor kid clapped his hand over his mouth and ran for home.

Near our secondary school, a weir had been built during the Depression, perhaps as a make-shift work program. The riverbank beside the weir was a great spot from which to watch the ice break up in the spring. Huge chunks of ice would crash over the dam, sometimes piling up one chunk on top of the other, all moving with a roar louder than a freight engine. If the ice didn't move along in a regular way, it could jam up enough to threaten bridges crossing the river. Jam or no jam, the ice break-up was greeted joyfully as a sure herald of spring and the end of the long prairie winter.

The Market Garden

I doubt that vegetable gardens are very interesting to most children — certainly they were not to me as a child or teen — but looking at gardens was an essential activity when we visited our relatives in southern Saskatchewan. Sometimes we were a bit dismayed at what we saw: some of the rows were crooked, some plants had been allowed to dry up, some peas or beans had gone to seed. Father's garden, on the other hand, was a model of straight rows, replanted spaces and perfect produce harvested exactly when it was ripe.

I remember in particular my Uncle Roy's garden. It barely survived on a bleak hillside, the plants seeming to grow any old way, volunteer potatoes sprouting up amidst the cabbages and puny pumpkin vines wandering into straggly stocks of corn. Not for display, this garden. We looked at it for as little time as possible and, as soon as we were dismissed, ran off with our cousins to play amongst several broken-down outbuildings that were connected to one another by crazily leaning fences. It all made a sort of maze. My little cousin Morris fell behind the rest of us and called for me to wait for him. I was last in line, because I was fat and didn't run very fast. Morris said, "Just wait a minute. I want to see if I can do this." What he was trying to do was to pee through a knothole in the fence — very fascinating to me who had no brothers. Certainly when I was six or seven years old, it was more interesting than looking at the peas and carrots.

A few years later, whether we were interested or not, my sisters and I learned to pay attention to a vegetable garden. These were the World War II years when the Canadian government promoted vegetable gardening as one way that ordinary people could help the war effort. Father had been a soldier in World War I, and in his own quiet way he was very patriotic. He decided that his three teenage daughters would plant a "victory garden." The soil on the Forestry Farm was first class, water was plentiful, and the city of Saskatoon would provide our market.

The three of us were shown a well-prepared plot of land that adjoined the road. It was government land, but we could use it since it was being put to a government-approved project. This is where we would plant our garden. Because it would be clearly visible to all passersby, Father made it abundantly clear to us that our garden would need to be a showcase in every way — well planted, meticulously weeded and carefully harvested.

Having been around gardens all of our lives, we had a pretty good idea of the process to follow. First we needed to line up a string the length of the plot and parallel to the road. No estimating here; the sticks that held the ends of the string were a measured distance from the road so that, with the string as a guide, we could make a perfectly straight shallow trench in which to plant the seeds. Father examined that trench: its width, its depth and especially its straightness. We tried hard to please him, re-working the row as required, widening it and lining it up until it was just right. Father stayed beside us as we planted the seeds, first those that would germinate early — radishes, green onions and lettuce — and later on beans that would produce very tender seedlings unable to survive the cold, early spring nights. A measured distance from that first row, we would dig the second trench, probably for carrots or turnips. The process continued until the whole plot was covered with row upon row of vegetable seeds.

Potato-growing involved a different procedure. Father presented us with shrivelled old potato tubers that had been preserved throughout the winter in a pail of sand in the cellar. Sprouts already emerged from the ancient skins. The trick was to cut these "seed potatoes" into pieces, each piece mothering a sprout. We set those pieces carefully in their own deep trench.

When the little plants began to emerge and the lovely straight green rows appeared, we felt proud of ourselves. All of that planting didn't seem to have been much of a chore. The weeding job lasted all summer, of course — Father taught us that a good weeder "moves all the soil" — but we took some pride in the look of our clean garden. In general, the gardening was just fine with us. But how we hated the marketing.

The preparation for the market days was rather fun. On two evenings each week, we would gather whatever produce was ready for use, clean it and then bunch or bag it. We would tie radishes and carrots in bundles of six or eight, set green or yellow beans in brown paper bags, and leave a great cabbage on its own, trimmed of any ugly outer layers. Then we would fill our marketing wagons: the baskets that were on the fronts and backs of our bicycles. Between the three of us, we could transport quite a respectable load of vegetables from our house to the city houses five miles away.

The packing and the bike riding were just work and we didn't mind that very much. Our parents gave us lots of advice and help and all of us had some input as to the pricing of our cargo. This preparation for market days was not a problem. It was the knocking on back doors and asking the housewives to buy our produce that spoiled the project for us.

The part of Saskatoon that was near the university was the closest to where we lived and comprised the homes of academe. There the residents recognized value and were careful with their dollars, making it a good place to sell fresh vegetables. We would ride our bikes along the back alleys and take turns knocking on doors. The ladies who emerged were nice to us but we did feel uncomfortable. I guess we felt like beggars. We should have been proud of our enterprise and pleased with the beautiful vegetables that we had to sell, but we weren't. We felt inferior. I came to hate one particular cabbage — large and beautifully green, but too big to be saleable for any one family's use. That cabbage traveled back and forth with us more than once.

Some women would ask us rather personal questions such as, "Are you girls Christians?" or "What does your father do?" We just wanted them to buy the great cabbage.

How good it felt to be cycling home with empty baskets and a few dollars in the common moneybag. Once — only once! — Jeanne, as the oldest, decided that we could treat ourselves to an ice cream cone from the corner store on our way home.

At the end of the summer we had amassed just slightly more than $50 each. Father encouraged us to buy war bonds and that's what we did.

Market gardening was a seminal experience that etched in my mind the conviction that, although I didn't mind physical work, from now on I would try to avoid being in a position that made me feel inferior to others.

I turned fifteen that summer, my hair was longer, I had grown taller and I was not fat anymore. I was not beautiful, but neither was I an ugly girl.

The Legacy of Religion

Our forefathers believed that happiness ultimately descended from God who kept a tally of merit points and rewarded his people either on earth or in heaven, according to their score. The highest grades were given for unshakable belief in God and Jesus Christ, and the next highest for obedience to certain moral precepts which were clearly set out in the Bible. This was my understanding of the way my grandparents viewed the road to happiness. My parents, though, were prepared to question the beliefs of their forebears and to step out from some of their inherited religious strictures.

To Mother and Father, religion had more to do with morality than belief. The beliefs were of an "own choice" kind: what made sense to them, they believed; what seemed to be untenable, they discarded. For instance, Mother made no bones about discarding the concept of the virgin birth. She had been a deaconess in Winnipeg's North End, an area of extreme poverty where she had worked with pregnant girls who could not or would not name the father of the child they were carrying and who would've been happy to have claimed to be virgins. Mother was proud, I think, to feel free to discard this tenet. (It seems to me that I was told about that before I knew what it was to be a virgin.) The resurrection was also an imponderable that they decided not to accept. My parents were not quite ready to give up on heaven — there must be something after death — but just what, where and how was too difficult a conundrum to be tackled; better to just get on with today.

A senior worker on the Forestry Farm was an atheist. My parents thought he was a lovely man and they rather pitied him for his unbelief, though they did not assert strong beliefs themselves. Father always said grace at dinner and supper, but he always used exactly the same words and said them quite without passion of any kind. I never saw either of them read the Bible and the Bible was never discussed. They had a great distaste, even disdain, for Pentecostals who were the evangelicals of their day and who were judged to be altogether too passionate about what, in Mother's and Father's eyes, was just there.

Although the absolute beliefs promulgated by the Protestant churches were not held by my parents to be prescriptive, there were moral certainties that were unquestionable. There seemed to be a lot of moral certainties, actually, pretty much based on the Bible's Ten Commandments and the beatitudes. That's where the Bible got it right. No drinking; using alcohol in any form was absolutely forbidden. No lying, and never any swearing. The overall rule seemed to be caution and common sense and love thy neighbour.

So what about Sunday school? Until I was eight years old, we did not even attend church regularly, let alone Sunday school. As with the case of socializing, location was a problem. There was no church within walking distance, no car was in use and work horses needed time to rest. When we moved to the Forestry Farm, however, Mother and Father started attending Westminster United Church in Saskatoon, where Great Uncle Tom and his family were pillars. It was a real effort even to go to the Sunday service there and it certainly would have required far too much devotion to have added another hour in order for the three of us to attend Sunday school. We were not anxious to do that anyway: it would've been yet another thing for us country mice to get used to.

A tragic occurrence changed all that: the Sutherland United Church burned down. Sutherland was a village situated about two miles from the Forestry Farm on the way to Saskatoon. All along, Mother and Father had felt guilty about being seduced by the city church and neglecting the country parish nearer home. With the small church now in great trouble with no building, they threw their support to it. Ah, then there was no reason why the girls should not join the party. The three of us must go to Sunday school.

It wasn't what I wanted to do. I didn't find it stimulating or even interesting, although there were some pretty publications on little cards and sometimes there were papers with stories and pictures of flowers and trees and Jesus. The minister's wife taught the class I was in. She was very sad because her only son had been killed early in the war, and she cried a lot. I felt very sorry for her, but I silently agreed with one of my classmates who dropped out of Sunday school saying, "Who needs to go there and watch her cry all the time?" Eventually there were so many dropouts that we were allowed to stop attending.

Not much of my spiritual journey was started in Sunday school and not much "at Mother's knee" either. However, I believe some personal development occurred because we emulated my parents as religious free-thinkers. If they could choose what Biblical prescriptions they would accept, so could we. They encouraged us to think for ourselves and to journey on with their blessing.

So how then did this fat little girl from Saskatchewan find happiness? I was no longer a fat little girl. I may have believed that I would be happy if I was a *good* girl, but I was beginning to wonder whether that was enough.

Aunt Minnie

Mother rather scorned Aunt Minnie, her brother's wife. Maybe that was because Aunt Minnie was a Pentecostal, which was worse than being a Catholic. Somehow the Pentecostals had a choice that the Catholics did not: if you were a Pentecostal you were foolish; if you were a Catholic you were unfortunate — you were born that way. In Mother's hierarchy of churches, the Pentecostals were a bit below the salt. When they were in church, some of the Pentecostals would shout "Hallelujah" or "Amen"; in our United Church only the minister shouted. The Pentecostals tended to sway a bit when they stood to pray or to sing the hymns; I wasn't even allowed to move my bottom around on the piano bench when I played "Jesus Loves Me." Their songs often sounded merry and were accompanied by a tinkly piano; our hymns were slow and steady, a bit of a drone with a strong bass line. We were four-square and stoical, whether in church or outside of it. Shows of emotion at any time, for any reason, were low class; you could cry in the woodshed on your own time.

Mother's scorn of Minnie could also be tied to her sister-in-law being "not good enough for my brother." Minnie was no oil painting, that's true, but neither was Uncle. He was bald early in life and he had an eye that veered off a bit so we didn't know whether he was seeing more or less than the rest of us.

One day when I was almost an adult, I learned that there was a lot more to Aunt Minnie.

Living conditions for her family were dismal. The farm was carved from prairie grassland that should have been left for those that thrived on the native wild grass — the deer, the antelope and the great buffalo herds. The soil, light and sandy, could not endure being broken into fields to grow wheat, oats or barley. Farming was a mistake. Once attacked and broken up by plows, the exposed topsoil was assaulted by the near constant summer winds that blew it into useless banks along the territorial barbed wire fences. Left alone, it would have been great ranch land; to farm it was disastrous.

The farmyard was thirsty for water, starved for trees or any greenness at all. It was a forlorn and wretched scene. There was no electricity, no running water, no motor for the washing machine or the milk separator. When I visited the farm, it was in the 1930s Depression. Odd. No one ever seemed to fall into a personal depression; hard times fell on so many people that no one could claim special depression status. Aunt Minnie certainly didn't.

Aunt Minnie canned (that is, preserved in jars) more saskatoon berries than Mother did. Far more. That's where she had it over Mother. But then, Aunt Minnie's saskatoon preserves lacked sugar and were not very tasty in themselves. They were quite wonderful, though, with the ice cream that was a special production of this house.

The men of the family, Uncle and his four great boys, would collect blocks of river ice and store them in sawdust in a small "house," really a pit dug into the side of a hill and covered with a roof made of scraps of lumber. The ice would stay frozen in there until midsummer. It wasn't needed in the long prairie winter days and nights, of course, but on summer afternoons it provided a marvellous social bonus. The farm produced lots of eggs and cream and there was an ice cream making machine — rather a simple gadget with a bucket and an inside cylinder in which the ingredients were assembled with lots of sugar included in *this* recipe. The kids took turns grasping the wooden handle and churning the cylinder about inside the bucket of ice until the ice cream magically developed. It was served to us in great porridge bowls and covered with saskatoon berry preserves. The mounded purple slush was very tasty. Father would eat two full bowls, to which Mother would say, "Oh, Tom!"

Accompanying the ice cream were large squares of white cake, decorated with pink, pink icing. I don't think the amount of food colouring got away on my aunt: she just liked the colour pink to speak clearly for itself. We called the particular shade of Aunt Minnie's icing "Minnie Pink."

When I was about fifteen years old, I stayed with Aunt Minnie and her brood for a couple of days. This home was a starved-looking 1930s house — a biscuit box, two storeys high, portioned into small square rooms except for the kitchen which was quite large. In most of the house, the floors were made of basic wide, plain boards, but in the kitchen there was linoleum — several layers of it, the new covering laid on top of the old ones, and that last layer worn down in some places to the second layer, and in some places to the first. Right in front of the kitchen counter all of the layers were worn away so that you could stand on the bare boards and look down between them into the basement.

Layering was a common practice and not just with linoleum. Paint, for instance, was slathered over worn window ledges and door jambs until it was as thick as icing, and new wallpaper furnished an extra bit of insulation when plastered over the torn and fly-speckled flowers of the previous layer.

The kitchen was by far the most important room in the house. In one corner there was a small stand, an upturned wooden apple box with a wash basin on it, a pail of water nearby and a dipper. Along one side of the kitchen slumped a spare-looking cot for the father's brief rest after dinner. (Dinner was always at noon.) A great oblong table filled most of the rest of the space. The wood stove served both for heating the whole house and for cooking. The kitchen became very warm in summer when the saskatoon berries were being preserved and the bread baked. In winter, water left in the wash basin might be frozen by morning.

Steep, narrow stairs led to the second floor and the bedrooms. Once at the top of the stairs, I knew I could not get down safely.

It was like climbing down a ladder frontward. And I did fall, though I wasn't hurt.

When I was directed upstairs to the little bedroom where I was to sleep, I was awestruck by what I saw. A princess could sleep there. The bedding, the pillows, the curtains were all white — a bright clean, clean white, every piece adorned with a lace border. The room was very small, but it was exquisite. I suppose that all of the linens were made of bleached flour sacks and that the lace was hand crocheted, but the contrast of this sweet little room to the otherwise depressing, bleak house and yard was startling. I didn't feel clean enough to stay there. "How you have been misjudged, Aunt Minnie," I thought. "How talented you are, how special!"

I didn't tell Mother that I thought Aunt Minnie was a special lady and that I liked her. Mother would not have wanted me to question her judgment of her sister-in-law. Neither Mother nor I was ready for that. But the event was another incident in the development of independent thinking and of questioning my childhood faith in all that I was taught.

Avery: Grandfather's Tractor

Avery should have been put into a museum. He was almost one of a kind: a huge, expensive behemoth of a machine, so large that a tall man could stand inside one of his wheels. I thought that Avery never moved, that he was stationed in one place and that whatever needed to be worked on was brought to him. Not so. Father claimed that he could have driven the tractor across Canada with the number of miles he had traveled on it working his father's fields. But Avery came to a grievous end. Father took him apart and donated his pieces as scrap metal for the war effort.

World War II had not affected us directly: Father and other people in his age group were too old for active service and my sisters and I were too young. Besides, the war was far away from North America, let alone Canada. But in the summer of 1940, Father became very worried when he listened to the news on the radio each evening. One time I heard him say to Mother, "You know, we just might not win this war." Father was determined to do his best as a passive supporter of Canada's war effort. That is why he volunteered to sacrifice Avery.

Father took me with him when he went to Grandfather's farm to dismantle Avery. I really can't remember why I was the one chosen to go on this trip, and it didn't seem to be a matter of my choice. If it had been, I would probably not have gone and I would have missed a salient event.

We traveled by train. The prairie countryside is a bit monotonous and I soon became bored. Father taught me how to estimate the speed of the train by counting the number of telephone poles that we passed in one minute. Counting poles: good way to pass the time. They seemed to go on forever, sentinels on the flat prairie land. At last we reached Alsask, a smallish town that straddles, as you might guess from its name, the border between Alberta and Saskatchewan. Grandfather met us at the station in his car and drove us the twenty or so miles to his farm. He ground the gears horribly. Grandfather never did really master the use of the clutch.

This was Grandfather's car, Grandfather's farm and Grandfather's tractor. Grandmother was there all right and she was a force to be reckoned with, but in her own home she was billed as Grandfather's wife. It wasn't that she was illiterate or shy; she was in fact a pillar in the local Women's Missionary Society and would take a leadership role there. But in her own home, Grandfather appeared to be the leader and that status did not seem to be questioned. (In my home, with Mother and Father there was a more even distribution of power.) Our cousins, who spent much more time than we did in our grandparents' home, have told me that this outward perception was not the real fact of the matter: behind closed doors, Grandmother made major decisions. When I

Avery: Grandfather's tractor

think about it, Mother probably agreed with the cousins' perceptions. She was not exactly a fan of Grandfather. He was far too paternalistic for her, far too autocratic. Indeed, this was one reason that she and Father made the unfortunate decision, just before the Depression, to buy their own farm rather than stay on Grandfather's homestead.

In Grandfather's home, each day started with a great breakfast of porridge, pancakes and eggs, followed by family prayers. Grandfather read from the Bible, after which all of us kneeled, facing our chairs, while Grandfather prayed for us. Some of the time, Father's brother or members of his family were with us and sometimes a "hired man," someone who helped with the farm chores. No one but Grandfather ever spoke a word; no one else ever talked to God and explained to Him how He should be looking after us that day. When Grandfather finished his business with God, he dismissed us from the family service and we scattered to our various stations.

Grandmother needed help to make the meals and keep the house in order. That's why I was there. While Father accosted Avery, I helped to "clear up," to wash dishes and, I especially remember, to pick and shell peas. I hated shelling peas. "Thank goodness," I thought, "we didn't have to shell the peas we sold from our market garden."

Every now and then I was allowed to watch Father make his assault on Avery. Father didn't talk much as he worked, taking apart rod by rod, cylinder by cylinder this icon of power that had figured large in his youth. Every now and then, Father would stand aside and look for a long time at the giant whose strength was diminishing little by little; then he would decide what the great machine should give up next. It was like a slow death, but Father made sure that Avery maintained his dignity so that he was never in danger of crashing to the ground; that he looked robust until the very last supports, the wheels themselves, were withdrawn. The conglomerate of disassociated pieces of metal no longer even hinted at the stateliness of that once proud icon of power.

Meanwhile, Grandmother encouraged me to go into the parlour and play the organ. The parlour seemed to be an almost sacred place in my grandparents' home. It was cold in there and the atmosphere was as cool as the temperature. Every inch of the small room was stuffed with untouchable objects. Were they ever dusted? Did anyone ever really look at them?

I had taken piano lessons for some years by that time, but I had never seen or used a pump organ. Learning to play that instrument was the kind of challenge I enjoyed and it made up for the housekeeping chores and the shelling of peas. Before Father and I left for home, Grandfather and Grandmother arranged a great hymn-sing to which they invited nearby aunts, uncles and cousins. Everyone gathered around the organ, adding their voices vigorously if not harmoniously to Grandfather's — in the lead, of course — as I kept pumping and playing that organ until the chorus was quite sung out.

The evening was intended to be a farewell event for Father and me, but perhaps it was more than that. Perhaps it was also a farewell to Avery, sacrificed for the war effort, now only a great heap of scrap metal near the barn.

Orpha's School

Orpha seemed to have picked me off the street in Shellbrook. I don't remember how or where we met, just that she appeared in my life and became one of my best-remembered buddies.

Our family had moved to the small town of Shellbrook in 1945, at the end of World War II, at the time of my seventeenth birthday and just after my secondary school finals. I was rather lonely because the friends with whom I had graduated were headed to university while I had to wait out this year until there was money enough for me to continue my education. In the springtime, life would become fully charged with my first romance, but this was quite unforeseen during the first summer after school when I was just mooning about and in need of a friend. Then Orpha appeared.

My friendship with Orpha lasted much, much longer than my attachment to that first boyfriend, Alfred. Not that this was insignificant. For one thing, he taught me to dance. Country dances abounded in the small community halls that dotted the countryside, halls built by the farmers and positioned beside almost every school. A group of us, seventeen to nineteen years old, followed a four-person band from one hall to the next on Saturday nights. We would jive to every number, never lingering in the cars, not smoking or drinking.

The dances lasted until two or three o'clock in the morning, so I would get home very late to find Mother waiting up for me with the heat of her worry and anger almost setting her aglow. I would remonstrate, explaining that we had come straight home after the dance ended, but she was still upset. I didn't like to see her anger, but I thought her worry was needless as I was only having fun and was completely innocent of wrongdoing. Shouldn't there be a commandment, "Thou shalt trust thy daughter"? Despite Mother's disapproval, the whole event would be repeated the next Saturday night with the same consequences.

One Sunday afternoon, Boyfriend and I rode our bikes on some trails through a nearby country field, he with a shotgun over his shoulder for attacking gophers or rabbits. He let me try it. With my first shot, I blew the head right off a rabbit whose body gyrated up into the air and then lay still on the dirt just ahead of us. I was horrified: I had an immediate picture in my mind of the dear little rabbits of the Thornton Burgess stories. I had known when we set out what the game was, but I refused to play it anymore and insisted on riding straight home.

Boyfriend soon flitted away to a prettier girl. I was devastated. Mother, though, was ecstatic at seeing the last of him. She had been terrified that I would not escape with my virginity intact or that I would settle for being a wife in a small town. Puppy love she might have called it, but I would say that teenage romance can be a sweet thing.

Meanwhile, while Alfred was finishing secondary school, Orpha had graduated from Normal School (the provincial teacher-training institution) and was waiting to start her teaching career in one of the rural schools about ten miles out of town. Orpha was not a pretty girl: she had an ungainly shape and a long face. Perhaps that was why boys didn't show any interest in her. But then, she didn't show any interest in boys either.

At that time, the rural schools opened soon after the middle of August. The city schools didn't begin their year until after Labour Day, but in the country there had to be accommodation for the days in mid-winter when the snow and the cold kept many of the children at home, unable to travel on the unplowed dirt roads that connected the farm homes to the schoolhouse. It was the law that schools had to be in session for two hundred days, so the rural schools were opened early in the fall and then the Christmas holidays were extended by at least two weeks.

In many communities one of the farm families would "board" the teacher, while in other districts the teacher stayed in a teacherage, a small house on the school property. That's what Orpha did. Living in a teacherage provided privacy and easy access to the school, but in exchange for the use of this residence, the teacher was responsible for the day-to-day maintenance of the school building. For one thing, the teacher might have to assume the duties of the janitor — not such a bad chore, because some of the older children would vie for a chance to help with the cleaning and thereby spend a little extra time with this special person, the teacher. As well as providing janitorial service, on cold winter mornings the teacher would light the wood fire in the school's round-bellied stove so that the building would be at least a bit warm when the children arrived.

Electricity and plumbing were still not available for the homes or schools in rural Saskatchewan. Lamps fuelled by coal oil were the norm for lighting and the outdoor privy served the plumbing needs, although in some schools there was a chemical toilet for winter use, housed in a closet at the end of the cloakroom. No running water, of course. Community members took turns delivering an urn of drinking water to the school.

Once the school year began, I would only see Orpha on weekends. She did not have her own means of transportation to travel from her school to Shellbrook and back again, so she needed to get a ride with the parents of one of her pupils. Many of these parents, all of them farmers, had a car by then, for the Depression days were over and cars and gasoline were not impossibly expensive. Offering the teacher a ride home was a rather special thing to do.

When she was home, Orpha and I would have great visits and she would tell me about her week in school. She seemed to really care about the children and would talk about the ones who were very quick to learn and the ones who weren't, and about the strange and unexpected things that some of them would do. Phyllis was the oldest, in grade nine and taking a correspondence course. The teacher was not expected to teach beyond grade eight, so Orpha would just help Phyllis get the curriculum materials from the Department of

Education and then see that she got her assignments sent in to be critiqued and marked by the employees in Regina. Phyllis thought of herself as teacher's assistant, and took upon herself the task of keeping the younger children in line.

There were thirteen of them in all, counting Phyllis. Stan and Harold, the Big Boys, were plodding their way through grade seven. They were mischievous, but they never really challenged Orpha's authority. She told me that on Halloween they had pushed over the outdoor toilet. She learned later that this was a widespread custom and for the Big Boys *not* to have tipped over the privy would have been to let the side down. When Orpha saw the felled toilet, she laughed with them, then said, "I guess there are only two people here that can put that thing upright again," so they just got busy and pushed it back into place.

Little Barry was in first grade, trying to learn to read. One day the older children told Orpha that he had pulled down his pants and shown them his bare bottom. She decided that she would have to strap him to maintain her reputation as a firm, fair teacher *with good discipline*. At recess time, she opened the top drawer of her desk, the regulation place for the weapon to be kept. Orpha felt sick. She held little Barry's hand and gave it a bit of a tap with the ugly piece of leather. Then she just told him to be a good boy and go on out to play. He didn't shed a tear. But Orpha did — in the teacher's closet at the other end of the cloakroom from the chemical toilet.

One Saturday in November Orpha asked me if I would help her with her Christmas concert. Orpha wanted me to accompany the children on the piano as they presented their various songs and dances that comprised the school gala held on the last day before school closed for the long Christmas holiday.

The Christmas concert was almost as great a test of the teacher's success as were the reading scores. For two weeks, all learning ceased while the concert items were rehearsed. I suppose the purists could justify using school time to prepare the concert (instead of working on reading and writing) on grounds that all of the arts were dealt with during that two-week period. Anyway, the community members required it. All of the children must have a part: singing, dancing, acting or reciting; walk-on parts or major solos. "The Teddy Bears' Picnic" was a favourite finale in which all could take part.

A valuable asset would be someone to accompany the singing and provide background music for the plays. I could do that. At that time, I played the piano fairly well and I could manage a pump organ like the one I had learned to play in Grandfather's parlour.

Father drove us to the teacherage. I was wearing the warmest clothes I owned and I don't think I ever took them off during the week I stayed with Orpha. It was the coldest week of my life. The teacherage and the community hall were built with only a layer of siding for walls, no insulation anywhere, and great open spaces around the windows and doors. Overnight, the water would freeze in our wash basin and during the day, the frost on the windowpanes would be half an inch thick. The only warm spot was within a yard of the stove in the teacherage or of the barrel-shaped "furnace" in the hall. No one complained.

Not only was there a piano in that hall but also a pump organ. I tried out the piano first. To my dismay, there was no sound at all when I touched and then banged the keys. It wasn't hard to find out what was wrong: the strings that attached the key extensions to the hammers were severed and so there was no way that hitting the keys would make the hammers hit the strings. No sound. Further examination of the piano led us to the saboteur's hideout — a mouse's nest. Yuck.

So what about the organ? The sound that the pump organ made was a result of air passing from the bellows inside the instrument through the various holes that were opened when the player pressed the keys. Foot pedals pumped air into the bellows. It all worked very much like bagpipes and the sound was a bit like bagpipes too. But not from this one. Like the piano, there was no sound at all. Air could not be built up in these bellows, for they were full of holes. Another mouse attack.

What was to be done? Orpha looked at me as if she thought I was not really trying hard enough. And of course I did have to try harder. I decided that the organ was a hopeless case, but I could do something about the piano. I used every piece of string Orpha could find, including the tape that was in the waistband of her pyjamas, to attach the ends of the keys to the hammers. Not quite all of the eighty-eight needed to be repaired, but it took a full day to fix the severed ones before the piano could be used for rehearsal.

It was great fun when the rehearsals began, although not without the occasional conflict. Phyllis had to be reined in a bit: just because she was MC did not give her licence to be as much in charge as she would have liked. The Big Boys refused at first to be shepherds in the mandatory nativity scene: they said they weren't going to wear those dumb dressing gowns that had been organized for their costumes. Little Barry kept wandering off from the teddy bears' picnic. And Orpha just about lost it when the whole cast of thirteen dissolved in giggles as they were being taught to line up for their final bows. I wasn't as supportive of the singing parts as I would have liked, having to be so very careful to play the piano gingerly at rehearsal so that the pyjama strings would not come apart during the real show.

On the big night, parents and friends crowded in, stomping the snow off their boots and greeting one another with warm Christmas smiles. The hall became very steamy as all of the bodies finally warmed the old place and the snow on outdoor clothing melted. The children were at the top of their game, enjoying every minute, and the applause from the audience was surely akin to that at an opening show on Broadway. The piano held out, although I lost middle C and F-sharp halfway through "O Canada." Orpha's Christmas concert was declared a great success. Best of all, she got a distinct nod of approval from the superintendent who had sat in the back row the whole time.

It did not occur to me then that I might some day become a teacher and that I would greatly covet the approval of the chief education officer. Spending time with Orpha as a teacher's helper did not entice me at all to join ranks with her. Working at the Christmas concert was fun, but what I wanted was to get busy with my own learning again. Little did I know that education, one way or another, would become a lifelong project.

Salad Days

It was a glorious time, my first year away from home. It wasn't that I had longed to break free or that I resented the confinement of being at home, but I was ready for more — more friends, more challenges, more fun. I was not in the least timid about setting out to a new life where I would make decisions for myself, where I would face intellectual challenges, where I would meet social hurdles. I was ready to partake of my "salad days"— my first course of life in my own world.

There really wasn't any reason to be intimidated anyway. I stayed in Saskatchewan Hall, the only women's residence at the University of Saskatchewan; my older sister was one of my roommates; and Great Uncle Tom's daughter Edith was the matron of the residence and, to boot, the Dean of Women. I found Father's name, Thomas Rowles, in the library where there was a plaque for each university student who had served in the First World War. That made me very proud of my name and encouraged me to make something of myself.

The men's residence, Qu'apelle Hall, was just across the road from the women's residence. The men took their meals in the dining room of the women's hall so there was good opportunity for the interaction of men and women. It was, however, soon after World War II when many of the men were veterans, using their Department of Veterans Affairs (DVA) credits to complete their education. These men were older than most of us and they were especially serious students without much time for socializing.

I was in a general arts program in which the classes were not difficult; it helped that I had learned in high school how to study and to keep up with my assignments. The only thing that worried me was that first year students were required to take a course in physical education, that nemesis of mine. But something quite marvellous happened. I had decided to take fencing, of all things: it being the most innocuous of the options and also not like gymnastics, so at least I didn't know that I couldn't do it. I found out that the major physical requirements for fencing were flexibility and speed; I thought I might have these. I learned about positions — salute, en garde — and about moves such as thrust, lunge, riposte, parry, retreat. It was fun. In fact, at the end of the session, in competition with all of the other members of the class, I managed second place. Is it possible that I was not an athletic moron after all? What an ego-booster this was. And of all things, in a physical education course.

No one that I knew was a slacker during the week; on week nights, we studied and worked on assignments. But we were certainly happy to have a date for Saturday night. Dates were simple events and not costly: we would be taken to a movie or just out for coffee. An especially great date that winter was to go tobogganing as part of a group of six or eight. An enterprising builder had created a marvellous toboggan slide on the banks of the Saskatchewan River, steep enough to be great fun — and even a bit frightening.

Toward the springtime there were various faculty balls. I was invited to the Arts Ball and the Aggie Ball. Somehow I had enough money to buy a long dress. (Such a gown was absolutely mandatory to attend a ball.) I got the cheapest one I could find and it did look cheap, but there were lots of cheap dresses and what counted was the excitement of being dressed up and going to such an event. There was dancing, of course, but first there was a formal banquet — another new experience for this farmer's daughter. I had to converse sweetly with my escort and at the same time watch my table manners in the new situation. I remember attacking with my fork the first olive I had ever met and seeing it skitter across the table at someone's surprised date. My face registered innocence.

Innocence was the nature of the dates: a quick good night kiss was all. For what seemed good reason then, there was a curfew at Sask Hall; the outer doors were locked at eleven o'clock on weekdays and twelve o'clock on Saturdays. A bright light was positioned over the entrance, so a fairly public kiss or hug was the limit. I did come in late twice, both my sister and the Dean of Women in some distress. I got the cold stare but nothing more.

This lovely year came to a crashing end when I suddenly became very ill with spinal meningitis. The resident nurse, diagnosing my illness as a mild case of the flu, ordered me to get into a bed in the infirmary at Sask Hall. There had been a flu outbreak and it was assumed that my illness was just another case. If not for my sister Jeanne, who broke the rules by coming to see me, I would have died. When she came into the infirmary and saw that I was very ill, she found a doctor who would come to the Hall. He dispatched me immediately to a quarantine room in the city hospital and plied me with sulpha drugs. Meanwhile, he decreed that the residence be quarantined. Imagine the shambles in the residence, with the end of classes and exams only three weeks away. Course notes and romantic letters were passed up to the windows in buckets and assignments were sent out by courier to sympathetic professors.

A man I'd been dating sent me a bouquet of flowers — the first purchased cut flowers that I had ever seen. These flowers were the first things that I focused upon through the haze of regaining consciousness.

Because my performance during the year had been good, I was granted a pass in all of my courses except French — which was, I suppose, a test case. I wrote that exam in the fall and made a first class mark. But the consequences of that illness were far-reaching; it was a long time before I experienced once more the joy of that year's salad days, days filled with new friends, new experiences and the happiness of learning just for learning's sake.

Happiness: The First Accounting

To be happy, I have been told, you need these three things: someone to love, something to do, and something to look forward to. The thesis could certainly be challenged: too simplistic, not universally applicable, or a concoction created from a limited point of view. Fair enough. But I have been writing about how a fat little girl from Saskatchewan found happiness, and this formula for what constitutes happiness seems to work for me, at least as I have remembered this part of my life.

I particularly like the formula because it casts the responsibility for happiness squarely upon one's own shoulders. Each item on the list appears to be achievable most of the time. Isn't there always a way to find someone to love? Can't one always find something to do? Isn't it always possible to build into life something to look forward to? Maybe not for everyone, and maybe sometimes not for me, but still I would like to reflect upon these three elements of happiness and how they were present in my life to the end of the salad days.

Mind you, at eighteen I certainly did not analyze the presence of the components and, indeed, at that time I had not heard of them. It was only several years later, when my world seemed to be falling in around my ears, that my dear friend Orpha suggested that I would have to pull myself out of my gloom and that this formula would help. It seemed to work. Orpha taught me that, when I was feeling out of sorts, I should think about those I loved, look for something more satisfying to do, or craft something to look forward to.

First then, the *Someone to Love*. Psychologists tell us that children who are denied love at birth and during early childhood are often scarred for all of their lives. Lack of the love factor is likely to have terrible consequences. With regard to this love, I had great good luck: I was born into a loving, caring family. It was not always a joyful family, but in "The Dirty Thirties" circumstances were not conducive to abounding joy. My parents didn't have much to look forward to during those seemingly endless years of the Great Depression. Father once said, "You know, after two or three years of drought, you think that the next year will be better, but after five years of hard times, you begin to wonder if conditions ever will be better." In those days a lack of joy was common, so it is not surprising that I don't remember my childhood as a particularly happy time. That didn't mean there was a lack of love, though. My sisters and I were always well cared for and well loved. As a child, then, I was well supplied with that first ingredient of happiness — *Someone to Love*.

Later, as a teenager, I began to awaken to the idea of having one special person to be a love partner and I did indeed have an introduction to this kind of love with that first boyfriend. But that event was as shallow as the encounters with boys at the University of Saskatchewan during my first year there. For the *Someone to Love* factor, I still relied upon my family and it was steadily provided by them.

What about the *Something to Do*? Going to school was what there was to do and what I thoroughly enjoyed doing. After the few ugly weeks at Caron with Miss York, I enjoyed being in school more and more. My sisters and I didn't have much social life because of our isolation at the Forestry Farm, so there was lots of time for school homework, something that I actually liked doing — not that I would assert that to any of my schoolmates! Mother told us that it was our job to do our schoolwork; it was her job to look after the house. Perfect.

There was something else that had to be done: this fat little girl had to become thin. When I found that I could control my weight, I had a great feeling of accomplishment and even of power. Losing weight was an achievement. This element of happiness, *Something to Do*, already had some qualifiers: it must result in a feeling of accomplishment or achievement.

The *Something to Do* part went wrong the year I was seventeen, the year I didn't go to school. I was pretty glum most of the time. My job was to continue to take piano lessons. I knew that I was not good enough to ever make piano playing my career and I did not enjoy making music enough to really pour my heart into practising. Not at all. I did not feel that it was getting me anywhere. The sense of accomplishment was lacking. Luckily, when I went to university the next year, I regained a blissful *Something to Do*.

And what about the last component of happiness, according to the formula? What about *Something to Look Forward To*? When I was eighteen, I looked forward to getting back to school. Looking further ahead, I wanted to be a married woman with a family. That's all. I was not at all ambitious to have a career other than to become a wife and mother. In that era, women who worked outside of the home were on their own, either because they were not married or because there had been a disaster in their marriage due to death or divorce. And so, like most other girls of my generation, I did not plan to have a career. Right then, I was content with what I had to look forward to: school.

So, the fat little girl from Saskatchewan had found happiness, had she? It was only later that she learned that happiness is complex and sometimes elusive.

PART TWO

BRANCHING OUT

The flower of the Dogwood Tree is the provincial emblem of British Columbia. The Dogwood is a small tree, well loved for the way it explodes with white blooms in springtime. Students in British Columbia's public schools receive a Dogwood Certificate when they graduate.

Becoming a Teacher

I liked to learn and I wanted to keep on going to school, but there just wasn't enough money. I had needed the whole summer to recover from the meningitis that felled me in the spring, so I had nothing to contribute to my fees and board for the next year. When Father realized at the end of August just how much money he would need to give me for my second year, he said, "That's a lot of money." That's all he said, but I was devastated. I suddenly felt that I had become an undesirably heavy weight that he could no longer bear. I cried all that day and all that night.

Had I returned to a bit of the madness that I had felt long ago — the first time at Caron when I *didn't* want to go to school, and now in Shellbrook when I *did* want to go? The sky was falling. What could I do?

No one knew what that paroxysm was all about; in my usual way, I did not tell anyone what was the matter. Instead, I plummeted to an impetuous decision: I decided then and there that I would take charge of my own life. I would change my university program from arts to education: in that way I would have a teaching certificate by the end of that second year and would no longer need to look to Father for support. I would look after myself. With that decision, my career was defined: I would become a teacher.

No one in the family challenged my decision, for I didn't ask for guidance or even discussion — and there was none. All of us knew that paying for accommodation at university was more than we could earn in the summer months and so this would be as good a time as any for me to declare my independence. Why not become a teacher and make that my career or become a teacher until I had enough savings to take some other training of my choice? After all, that's how Great Uncle Tom's offspring had acquired their doctorates and their great careers — by teaching until they could find their own way to continue their education. So what was there to fuss about? I'd better just get on with my plan and be off for one more year to the campus that I loved.

The year did not begin well. My older sister became very ill with poliomyelitis, a dreadful, crippling disease that was endemic in 1947. At that time, there was no vaccine to ward off polio and there was no cure for it; the disease had to run its course. Jeanne was taken to one of the hospitals in Saskatoon that had a clinic with a good reputation for success in treating polio, but that clinic had only limited success with my sister's. After spending the whole long winter in hospital, first recovering from the immediate trauma of the disease and then under-going rehabilitation for its wasting residue, she was weak and lame by the time she was released from hospital in the spring.

I was the only family member living in Saskatoon and visited Jeanne every few days. I was not only devastated for her sake, but also horrified for the pain my parents had suffered because of my frightening bout with meningitis and now my sister's much worse attack of polio. It was heartbreaking to watch my sister suffering, the sorrow exacerbated by her courage and indomitable spirit. This was my first encounter with real grief.

At the same time, the education program at the University of Saskatchewan was extremely disappointing — not challenging and not even interesting. For the most part, the professors seemed tired, without sparkle or enthusiasm, and they presented their drab courses without demanding either ingenuity or effort from the students. They lectured from carefully numbered, dog-eared filing cards with no dis-cussion or challenge from the students. (We must have been a bunch of dolts, too.) If only the lessons had been enlivened by some anecdotes about students or teachers. Could it be that these instructors didn't really like teaching? I harboured a suspicion that they never *had* taught in the school system.

It was, however, during this depressing year of education courses that I found my teacher mentor, a professor who was a recently retired elementary school principal. Now, he *had* been a teacher! How strange it was that, though much older than me and without the charisma that I might have been looking for, he was inspirational enough that I began to believe that there could be excitement in helping children to learn. There could be magic. He convinced me that real enchantment could be embedded in the teaching profession.

This unexpected star shed his light on particular tenets that became basic to my work. The instruction that I remember from him was not a specific "how to," but an all-embracing "must do." He was passionate when he told us that we must never allow ourselves to dislike a student. How many times since then have I argued that point with my peers and how many of them have ever agreed that this is a possible goal? Hardly a one, and yet I think this is one of the greatest principles I ever followed as a teacher. It is possible to never allow yourself to dislike a child; moreover, I would say that a teacher can and must find something to like in every child.

My mentor also warned us that we had no business making ourselves so popular with students that they would not be ready to accept another teacher. I took that instruction to heart, too. I believed him when he said that our job is to help children to learn, not to love us.

When we education students mingled with students in other faculties, we would find ourselves being defensive about our programs. Our courses were Mickey Mouse, they would say. And they would quote the old adage, "Those who can, do; those who can't do, teach." I have since read with dismay that research in some colleges shows that those enrolled as education majors rank significantly below other professional majors in measures of scholastic achievement, intelligence and grades, and that there is a strong negative relationship between measured academic ability and retention in the teaching profession. So, it wasn't just that the courses were not challenging or interesting: it was us. We were just not very bright, apparently. Hmm. So what comes first: the boring teacher-training programs that attract low-achievers who can only survive by becoming teachers, or the poor image of the teaching profession itself so that only the mundane are attracted to the job? At the time it was better not to ask those questions, just move on.

Once the soul-destroying months of lectures were over, practice teaching sessions followed. When I joined a primary classroom full of children and their teacher, I did find the magic. I found that there is magic when small children learn to read. At first they only learn to remember sounds and words, but then comes a moment when they are suddenly aware that they have broken the code. They are no longer remembering words or sounds: they are deciphering on their own what is on the written page. The enchantment in their eyes is a joy to see. They love to sit beside you, to push against you so that you can both look at their special book and they can show you how accomplished they are with their newfound skill. You share in their epiphany.

For one small child that I met, the discovery of the Pogo books was delicious. She would hang around at the end of the school day, knowing that my appetite for Walt Kelly's comedic world matched hers, not knowing that I was listening to it at a different intellectual level from hers. She wanted to read and giggle for as much time as I would spare for her. Here was the bliss of being a teacher.

Watching the children interact on the playground was often intriguing. One day I overheard a forthright boy in second grade tell one of the girls in the class that she was ugly: "You are as skinny as a blade of grass." She may have been skinny and she certainly had no discernible hips, but she could keep a hoola hoop circling her little body for the whole of the fifteen-minute recess time. She tried to teach me but I never did get the knack. I was able to jump rope with the kids, though, and enjoyed it as much as they did.

I was assigned to a class of seven and eight year olds where the children would enter the classroom as soon as they got to school. Respecting the teacher's need to be at her desk, they would sit down at theirs and begin to work independently. When everyone had arrived or the bell rang, whichever happened first, the teacher and children would start the day's lesson together. It was a lovely situation that made me proud to learn to become a teacher.

The practice teaching weeks were ones when the university professors traveled about, assessing the student teachers who were in the front lines honing their skills in the classrooms. We had to perform in front of these grey-headed ones sitting at the back of the classroom, peering at us over the top of their glasses. What great luck I had: the professor who came to see me teach was the one that I thought of as my mentor. He agreed with me that I was being guided by a teacher who was a master of the craft, that this was the best learning experience I could have and that I should pursue this kind of excellence.

Becoming a teacher was not an easy feat for me, but in time it became my joy and my sustenance. I expect that there are "natural teachers." I was not one of them. I kept searching for a golden key that would open a door and show me a room full of glorious ways to fill every moment of the teaching day with inspirational learning devices. Instead of finding a golden key, I seemed to stumble along like a dullard during the first years of my teaching career; it was a long time before I really enjoyed my work.

Eventually I gained confidence and skill. For the most part, I did not learn to become a teacher by attending lectures or workshops; I learned to teach by watching master teachers at work and from experience.

Here was my *Something to Do*. I concluded, however, that this element of my happiness formula needed to be parsed further, to be analyzed carefully. I didn't enjoy teaching at first and my work did not help me to be happy. I did have something to do, but it wasn't until I could do it well that it became part of my happiness. I questioned my conviction about this particular element of happiness.

Meanwhile, the *Someone to Love* needed attention.

A Broken Dream

I had not really wanted to be a teacher: I had wanted to be a married woman. Now where did that idea come from? Certainly not from Mother. She was determined that all three of her girls must have a career, must never find themselves in a position where they were dependent upon a husband. She had her way: all of us have had thriving careers. She hadn't counted on the careers interfering with marriage, as they probably did. As it happened, only one of her girls ever married (the fact that the one had two marriages didn't really add to the count) and none had a biological child. Too bad. Some good genes may have been suppressed.

No, not from Mother came the desire to be a married woman. And events in the lives of two particular married women that I knew might also have discouraged that idea. Both of these occurrences were embedded in the war years, the first through the son of an acquaintance of our parents who was attached to the Commonwealth Air Training Scheme based in Saskatoon. He visited us a number of times when I was about fourteen years old. Eventually he married and brought his new bride to be assessed. I expected her to be as dashing as he was, but although she was probably very nice, I didn't find her attractive, probably because she was fat. She failed the test of comparison with the bride incarnate, Betty Grable — not that she asked for her grade. As it happened, our friend's son was killed by walking too close to an air craft propeller. Not a good scene all round. Nor was the second instance of what at first sight looked like married bliss.

When I was seventeen, the year I was waiting to go to university, I taught piano lessons to the children of a young mother whose husband was in the army. I knew that she had been living in some poverty throughout the war years, struggling along raising her three children by herself. Now that the war was over, she was eagerly awaiting her soldier's return. I thought her longing for him was romantic and that he must be a woman's dream. He was not. I met him when Father and I took my older sister to university in Saskatoon. Along with a farmer friend of Father's, this creep in gentleman's clothing caught a ride with us for the hundred-mile journey back home to Shellbrook. There had been heavy rain the night before, so that the back roads were slippery. Father, who knew these back roads well, could not keep the car on the track and off we went into a ditch. Only a tractor would get us back on the road. Father and the farmer, the front seat passenger, set off to get help, leaving me in the back seat with the returning soldier, the long-awaited husband of the sweet mother of my piano pupils. As a blushing seventeen-year-old, I was no doubt candy to him. Blackguard. He was trying to kiss me when my father and the other one returned. Still innocent and not classifying men as perfidious, I was nonetheless disenchanted about the romance of that couple.

No, the ideal of wife and mother did not seem to have emerged from the real world. It could only have sprung from the stories in the novels that I had read, the same ones that helped to instigate my get-thin project. L.M. Montgomery's "Anne books" were certainly influential — so out-of-date now and so irrelevant, yet so powerful to dream with when I was a fat girl in Saskatchewan. In *Anne's House of Dreams*, the fourth book of the series, Anne marries the boy who had teased her mercilessly in her primary school years. Even now I can picture Anne in her white picket-fenced cottage, her house of dreams, her astonishing, once scorned red hair piled high on her head; her slim, once skinny body enhanced by a colourful cotton frock; her shapely, once bowed legs set upon high-heeled white pumps. As you can see, my idea of marriage was immature — about one inch thick.

Not wanting to be a teacher and yet having to earn my own living, the great escape would be marriage. As a university student, being

escorted to various balls and coffee sessions did not lead to many pro-
posals of marriage, so at age nineteen, wanting immediate deliverance
from life as an unmarried school teacher, I accepted the first proposal
that came my way.

I regretted it at once. I didn't even tell my roommate that I was
"engaged." But neither would I go back on my promise. I remembered
well that Mother had told us how devastating it is for a man to be
encouraged by a girl and then dismissed. I believe this had happened to
her favourite brother: he was spurned by his sweetheart and never fully
recovered. High sin, that, and never to be countenanced by Mother
from any of her girls. What could I do? Marry him.

Fiancé was okay. He was a war veteran and so a little older than
me, fairly good-looking, mild mannered and obliging. His parents liked
me and I liked them. The ingredients were there, but they did not
blend well for me: the romance was just not evolving. Give it time, I
thought; try harder.

We had the idea that I would teach in Saskatoon while Fiancé
worked on the two years he had left to finish his degree in education.
We had to abandon that idea when we found out that the Saskatoon
city school board did not hire newly minted teachers, so I went home
to my own district where I could easily get work. Already, the dream
was imperilled.

I was dispatched to a school in Big River, a town at the end of the
railroad that runs to the northwest of the settled part of Saskatchewan.
Big River is surrounded by the northern boreal forest and hundreds
of lakes. The village was formed as a company town that was a centre
for the lumber industry, but by the time that I was a teacher there, its
economy was based on commercial fishing, mostly of Northern White
Fish. By its isolation at the end of the railroad and by its one-industry
status, Big River was a frontier town. Most young men and women
tried to escape, if they were not already caught up in its shallow, rough,
unpromising life.

Toward the end of my teaching year there, I got to know the bush
pilots that flew into the camps on the northern lakes, picking up great
buckets of white fish and bringing them in to the Big River cannery.
One of the pilots took me with him on several occasions when he was

going on a Saturday run. All that could be seen for miles and miles was forests and lakes. The assignment was to duck down onto a small lake where a couple of men would hoist into the small plane a great bucket of fish. Sometimes someone would beg a ride to Big River. It was not all right with the fish company for there to be hitchhikers, as there was no insurance for passengers — including me. But then, although these were not salad days, they were invincible days. No harm would come to us. Well, harm did come to me but not from falling out of the sky. As I found out later, the harm was in the seduction of the rarefied atmosphere.

The children in my grade five and six class comprised mostly sons and daughters of the fishermen. Perhaps today they would be classified as having one-parent status, for the fathers were away fishing most of the time. The women were lonely and isolated or else they lived lives of noisy, not quiet, desperation.

I made every beginning-teacher mistake there is. Classrooms in that school tended to be isolated fortresses; doors were closed and what went on inside the enclosure was a matter between the teacher and her pupils. I neither sought nor got help from other teachers. I wanted to keep my inadequacies to myself. The principal, whose classroom accommodated him as a waiting room for his retirement, left me to my own devices. He took various secretive smoke breaks — as we all knew — in the boiler room. I don't believe he was charged with the improvement of instruction in my classroom: that classroom was a laboratory where I had to find my way by trial and error. It was my nature to work hard and I expected the children to work hard too. That was my saving grace. I was a teaching acolyte, learning by immersion.

The year's experience in Big River opened my eyes mightily to the challenge of teaching and also introduced me to a different social life: straight ahead and at full throttle. Little by little I became very sad at the thought of marrying the dull, conventional, good man to whom I was engaged. When Fiancé visited me on long weekends and at holiday times, I would be anxious to see him and then, almost as soon as we were together, I would wish that we were not.

There were epic letters from him, quoting poetry and declaring exorbitant love for me, letters so long that they looked like bundles in their bulging envelopes. In novels, women whose hearts had been broken tied their love letters with pink ribbons and put them in their underwear drawer. I didn't keep mine. Even sheltered in my own bed-room, I was embarrassed to be reading those love letters. Could these be genuine romantic missives? Who was this creature Fiancé was extolling? No one that I knew.

Fiancé also sent me chocolates — a box each week. Now, for someone who was no longer a fat girl but who still had nightmares about the possibility of returning to such a state, chocolates were not romance enhancing. I jettisoned the ones I could not give away. Result-ing in guilt. Already guilt and much more to come.

When I went home at the end of June, I was drying dishes one evening when Mother said, "Well, it's time now to start planning this August wedding." I burst into tears. I held the dish towel over my face and sobbed into it. She rescued me at once. "My dear, if that's the way it is, we will just stop it now." And she did.

The experience of living in Big River and of breaking my promise to marry churned within me for a long time. On the one hand, in Big River I had ventured into a new way of life, a life that may characterize frontier people who live in the moment (as counsellors now tell us we all should do). There was some planning, yes, to avoid freezing to death or going hungry, but thinking or worrying about more than basic needs seemed unnecessary and unprofitable. People in Big River just *lived*, looking after themselves and their families, being kind to neighbours when the need arose, but not reaching beyond the boundaries of the town itself. I was deeply rooted in my upbringing, with the belief that self-fulfillment would come from achieving the best that I could be. But for a year I had been immersed in a morass of instant satisfaction, the pleasures of the moment, the joys of leaping and running. I knew that this was not the place for my life, but when I left it, I landed with a thud. I no longer knew what to do with myself or where I wanted to be. And I had to live with the dreadful hurt I had inflicted on someone who seemed to love me.

It was a long time before I found the *Someone to Love* and the *Something to Look Forward To*. This was a time of the lost happiness of the girl from Saskatchewan.

Dodging Boredom

Not knowing who I was or where I wanted to be, I drifted along without much passion for anything. Flotsam. The superintendent of schools had given me a recommendation for a place in the Saskatoon school district, a favoured destination for a young teacher who did not have ties to a particular rural community. For three years I taught in a school in the city, almost becoming one of the many single women who spent their lives teaching in the same school, sometimes in the same classroom for all of their working years. Security abounded. Passion did not.

A lovely lady in the classroom beside mine taught me what I needed to learn about working effectively with beginning readers. Even now I believe that she was a master teacher and that I was privileged to have her as a mentor. Still, she had taught the same way for twenty years, and the thought of spending my life that way was stultifying. This was not a time when teachers were encouraged to be innovative: the goal was to maintain the status quo. Teachers wanted to be considered professionals, but perhaps wanted even more to be considered philanthropists. Change was not encouraged. By the end of my second year I was bored. My teaching time in Saskatoon was not very rewarding; these were years of professional discontent.

Teachers lived very simply indeed, no one expecting to own a house or a car. While I taught in Saskatoon, another teacher and I rented two rooms in a house where six people shared one bathroom.

We cooked our meals on a two-burner hotplate and made up our bed each evening from the chesterfield in our "living room." We traveled by bus and streetcar. Since that time, the standard of living in Canada has increased enormously and the relative wages for teachers have undergone a sea change. But during my Saskatoon teaching days, even when I lived quite frugally during the school year, there was not enough money left over for summer travel or for self-indulgence.

I decided that, even though the teaching was tedious, my life didn't have to be. I worked away at completing my bachelor of arts degree, taking courses during the winter evenings and the summer holidays. That was interesting and challenging. (Bachelor of arts courses were a different genre from the depressing ones leading to a bachelor of education.) One winter I took two courses, madness to be sure. I didn't get very good marks, but I didn't get bored either. I realized that I was in a slump and that I would have to get myself out of it. The university, a place I loved, resuscitated me.

And then, of all things, I also joined the air force reserve. Father was furious. He told me that I would not be treated with any respect at all and that I had better get out of the reserve at once. Father was seldom so direct. He must have been remembering another era, for I was never treated without respect — although I do recall that as I reported to one of the officers when I was leaving the reserve, he looked me over and said, "You should *never* wear a uniform." None of the other teachers in my school thought this air force reserve idea was worthy of me, somehow, and my two close teacher friends were aghast. Nobody cut me socially because of this venture into the military, but some people rolled their eyes a bit as if I were doing something really abnormal.

By working as reservists on Sundays and one evening a week throughout the winter, teachers could supplement their meagre salaries and have a little fun. We could also be employed by the military during the summer holiday months. The possibility that we might be required to go to war never even entered my head. I recall wondering how the Canadian government could afford to pay us for the very little bit of work that we did.

We could also go to the reservists' summer camp. Now that was an adventure. The first summer I was in the reserve, our squadron went to Whitehorse for two weeks. Whitehorse is so far north that in the summer the sun rises only two or three hours after it sets. Some evenings we sat on a log far above the camp, watching one day end and another begin. I was in the good company of former members of the Royal Canadian Air Force whose experiences were varied and whose conversation was lively.

Once we were back on the base again, I spent some lovely evenings in the company of a young air force fellow. Being a university student meant he was classified as an officer. He took me into the officers' mess once or twice and then found some other place for us to spend time together. I concluded that he had been asked not to bring me into the officers' lounge because of my non-commissioned status. Funny feeling, to be excluded because I didn't rate. I didn't tell Father.

The sunsets we watched that summer still flash through my mind's eye when I think of the prairie. Big sky country indeed: surround colour evening after evening. At the end of the summer, my officer friend transferred east to the University of Toronto. I had arranged to leave Saskatoon also, but to travel west, not east. I remember him fondly, but had no regrets when we parted, for it was never more than a summer interlude for both of us.

I made the great escape from the Saskatoon teaching assignment, escape from work that I did not do very well or like very much, escape from a life that was only occasionally vibrant, escape from the prospect of being the same, same, same in twenty years. The money in my pension fund would see me through a year at the University of British Columbia. Good decision. It was a bold move, away from the safety of assured work and good friends. I was twenty-two.

To British Columbia — Aha!

The drive to the University of British Columbia (UBC) was my introduction to Vancouver. I had never seen anything so beautiful, so grand. Great trees bent to touch one another above the avenues and gorgeous hydrangeas vied for attention along the university boulevard. My joy in living in British Columbia began then and there and has never left me.

Some people may tell you that, during the winter months, the rain on the British Columbian coast will drive you mad. It doesn't drive me mad. In Saskatchewan, to avoid the killing cold we would calculate to the minute the time we had to be outside. In BC, I could always slog my way from here to there in relative comfort under an umbrella, wearing sturdy shoes or boots. For me, with freedom from the domineering prairie climate came freedom from other kinds of confinement: the bondage of work and the pressure of years passing by in a physically and socially flat environment. I am so glad I recognized the need for change and so happy to have had the good fortune to moor in BC.

My first home in British Columbia was on the UBC campus, which was undergoing growing pains. Space for residences and classrooms had been adapted from military camp quarters and offices — a temporary arrangement that continued for many years. The room I shared with another student was roughly put together, but it had its own shower, a luxury compared to the rooms I had rented in Saskatoon. Meals were provided in another army hut. Many students complained about the institutional food; I was mum, not wanting to appear too plebeian by admitting that I actually enjoyed the food.

That September, walking half a mile from one hut to another for history or English classes expanded my soul. Except for the recycled army huts, UBC has a beautiful campus with some charming old buildings. I took time to absorb the lovely old library with its clock and bell tower. I would like to have stayed forever. Well, I almost did — there were gaps between some of the learning spasms, but I was a student there off and on until I was sixty-three years old. But that story will come later. This first spasm would last for two years, during which I completed a bachelor of arts degree and accrued credits toward a bachelor of education.

The course of salad days at the University of Saskatchewan had been consumed five years earlier. Now here was the entrée. I revelled in my history and English courses, studied steadily and felt at peace.

The summer between those two years, however, was disastrous. I needed to work that summer in order to stretch my finances for a second year at UBC. My friend Betty and I got jobs at a huge hotel in Banff, Alberta, where we were set to work folding sheets and table-cloths in the laundry. These linens were fed one at a time into the first of four huge mangles that they then traveled over and under, being dried and pressed as they wound their way through the crush. As each item emerged from the last mangle, Betty and I would each grab a corner and fold the steaming linen according to a set procedure. The process became something of a dance routine where we moved out, forward and back, folding the sheet or tablecloth until it formed a neat package that we slapped onto the table beside us, then grabbing the next item before it crumpled or fell. We discovered that the boss was turning the machine to a faster pace as we perfected our dance steps. What a sweatshop! It was a hot summer and we were performing very close to those hot, hot rollers. I had never in my life done such physically demanding work.

That work came to a crashing end, when I was in a serious car accident — a head-on collision. A man in the other car was killed and the passenger beside me in the front seat suffered a broken hip.

My right foot and knee were badly broken. The doctors skewered the broken bones of my foot onto rods — like kebabs — and patched the knee as well as they could. Mother and Father were told about the accident by a friend who heard about it, including my name, on the radio. Don't the police withhold information about accidents "until notification of the next of kin"? Once again my poor parents were shocked to learn that one of their daughters was in physical distress. But it wasn't as bad as they feared.

I spent six weeks in the aging Banff hospital while my foot and knee mended enough that I could get around on crutches. I was able to hobble back to UBC in September, relying on crutches for most of the winter but eventually able to walk without even a limp. With the help of borrowed money, I continued my UBC studies for a second year.

These two shining years were enhanced by the companionship of an engineer who had come back to school as I had after several years in the workforce. We became buddies and spent many hours walking to classes, meeting for coffee, going to parties. (Engineers are great party-goers.) Our enjoyment, perhaps I should say love, of one another was bittersweet. My friend failed his year and then failed it again the second time round. Meanwhile, my program was as easy as pie. He would say, "You're a smart little buddy. Too bad I'm not." I kept assuring him that my classes were much easier than his, which they were, but it is not good when a woman appears to outstrip a man. Funny how the other way around seems to be acceptable. After two happy years, our relationship cooled. Time to move on.

While my engineer and I were preparing to go our separate ways, a teacher had been striving to court me. This was Robert Leullier, and now I quickly married him. My parents and sisters were well-pleased to welcome this new family member and to see me setting out into married life with the prospect of the home and family that they knew I wanted.

Robert and I bought a house in the beautiful Fraser Valley where both of us continued to work at our teaching careers. I was no longer a little fat girl and I no longer lived in Saskatchewan, but the happiness quota was still not altogether in place.

Tudor: House of Dreams

Not at all like Anne's House of Dreams — a small cottage with a white picket fence — our house was a bit of a landmark, established on a main road near Cloverdale in Surrey. Of a pseudo Tudor design, it was a rather ancient house that sat on top of a hill. I liked Tudor's exterior design as well as its interior: a large country kitchen, a cozy retreat room with a wood fireplace, even a scary attic that reminded me of the house at Caron. It was a grand place for nest building. We set about painting walls, making drapes, buying furniture and then hosting our relatives and friends.

Even more precious than Tudor itself were the eight acres on which it stood, most of them covered with trees. An acre had been cleared for the garden and orchard.

This idyll did present an immediate, unexpected challenge: to our dismay, a day or so after we encamped we were confronted with a water problem. Only a little bit of the precious liquid dribbled out of the taps and the little bit that did appear was a nasty, brownish colour. Something had to be done about that, and quickly. Aside from our own personal needs, there were some special demands for water. We had some projects on the go.

The first project was to attend to the fruit that we had picked as soon as we had moved into Tudor — a pail full of cherries to be preserved in jars and stored for making pies during the winter. Cherries are not a cooperative fruit: they must be picked as soon as they are ripe, which is why we did so at this awkward house-settling time, and

Tudor, 1960

once the cherries are picked, they will not stand for any waiting about until they are properly preserved. Cherry preserving is a very labour-intensive job and it is a very sticky job. The procedure involves pitting each cherry with a special tool. The cherries are placed one at a time onto a small indented spot on the cherry-pitting tool, then a plunger forces out the pit, leaving the gutted cherry behind. We possessed both a hand-held pitter and a table model, but each tool needed both hands of the wielder who could pit just one cherry at a time. As you can imagine, it takes many pitted cherries to fill a jar. The seemingly endless sticky, sticky job demands more water than the little dribble of muddy-looking stuff that was emerging from our taps.

There was another special demand upon our water supply. We had bought a young calf — a steer — that was intended for our winter's meat after it was fattened throughout the summer on the good-looking grass in a cleared section of the yard. In case either of us might succumb to the calf's charms and foolishly make a pet of it, we named it "Sirloin." There was to be no doubt about its purpose. As far as I was concerned, there was really no need to worry about becoming fond of Sirloin. I disliked him almost at once, mostly because he commandeered our precious water. He also bawled a lot.

As it happened, I was left alone to cope with the water situation. When we first occupied Tudor, picked the cherries and bought Sirloin, it was at the end of the school year. Robert, who was a secondary school teacher, had volunteered to mark examination papers in Victoria, BC's capital city. Many of our colleagues readily took on this task in order to earn a little money to add to their frugal incomes. Robert and I had agreed that he would go to Victoria for this two-week stint, and that I would be in charge of the new property, preserving the cherries and looking after the calf. But we hadn't counted on the water problem. We only realized that there was a problem just before Robert left home, when he tried to have a bath and instantly became aware of the drought.

We concluded that the problem was with the ancient pump that brought the well water into the house, so as Robert left home we agreed that I should call a plumber. The plumber, though, had several other tasks to attend to before mine, so there would be no help until the following day. Meanwhile, Sirloin started to bawl and the cherries looked more and more depressed. What on earth should I do?

I thought about my good farm roots and told myself to get on with it. I was able to take the top off of the well, find a rope and a pail, and haul up a bucket of water. Then another one. In almost no time, the calf was less angry with me, and as I laboured over the cherries they began to fill the jars little by little. When the plumber arrived the next morning, he explained that there was nothing wrong with the pump at all; the problem was with the pipe that was meant to carry the water up to the surface. The pipe was not long enough to extend down to the last two feet of water left in the bottom of the well. What I needed to do, he explained, was to buy a tank of water.

It was not really a surprise to find that the trucker who brought the tank knew the property very well. He had been providing water for Tudor for some years. Hmm.

The cherries made the greatest pies ever. As for Sirloin, although he never became a pet, we still did not eat him. He didn't seem to be gaining weight — and yet he was in the middle of a field of green grass. Grandfather came to stay with us for a few days and told us that it was quack grass and that cattle do not eat that kind of grass. No wonder Sirloin bawled: he was starving. We felt remorseful and got rid of our guilt immediately by selling the calf and buying a rotor-tiller to help us make the grassy plot into a larger garden and orchard.

We did try a bit more animal husbandry: we bought a half dozen bantam chickens to keep in a small shed at the edge of the clearing. My penchant for bantam chickens had stayed with me from when I had admired them at the Moose Jaw Fair that time when we escaped from both the great bull and the pretty ladies sideshow.

These bantams didn't survive. Before we even knew them well, one after another was absent at roll call for their morning treat. Early one day we saw a flash of a bushy, almost apricot coloured tail. Undoubtedly it was attached to a fox just disappearing into the bushes. I thought of Reddy Fox of the Thornton Burgess stories of my childhood. Inevitably, in this real adult world, our bantams disappeared one by one. Although we never did see the fox again, we were sure enough that he was responsible for this second disappointing venture. One way or another, we just did not seem to be successful farmers.

There were birds and animals, however, that visited us in their own time. We came to expect proud, raucous Stellar's Jays to pass through when the filbert nuts were ripe. And one time a possum tried to fool us into thinking he was ill or dead when we came upon him under the plum tree; we called the dog away and, as we hid behind the garage, he stopped "playing possum" and slunk off. Starlings, very unpopular, came year after year to nest above the garage doors, depositing rivers of white excrement all over the beautiful wisteria.

A great weeping willow tree guarded Tudor's west side — probably stationed there when the house was first built. Its yellow-green leaves softened the sturdy structure of the house and graced the flower beds below. We were astounded to hear from Robert's brother that the tree had to go. "Have you any idea what harm those roots are causing to the driveway? See how the cement is heaved? And it is clear that the drainage tiles around the house are blocked because of the condition of the basement floor. It has to go."

I mourned the demise of that beautiful tree, and Tudor looked as if he'd had a bad haircut.

The garage listed to an alarming degree. It had been well and tastefully built, but now it looked defeated, disconsolate. After some conferencing, the diagnosis was for surgery — corrective and cosmetic. The garage was made to stand tall again and gradually became quite beautiful as, in time, a lovely soft pink rose bush and a flamboyant Japanese quince covered its scars.

Tudor presented other problems associated with an ancient house: a leaking roof, clogged drainage pipes, cracks here and there in the corners of rooms. His leaks and cracks could be mended, but unfortunately they had also started to appear in the marriage which, although it survived for more than twenty years, did not thrive and eventually fell apart. Tudor had provided a necessary, but incomplete, "House of Dreams." In time, he succumbed to the wrecker's ball and the eight lovely acres were strewn with a dozen houses for suburbanites.

Wayne

I found Wayne in my classroom when he was seven years old. He was living in a foster home near the school where I taught, and I learned that the Children's Aid Society that had placed him there was going to move him again. Robert and I petitioned the Society to have Wayne move to our home. They were delighted to do so. After he had lived with us for a few weeks, we applied to adopt him, signed the required papers and he became our son. In the end, it is a bittersweet story: Wayne died when he was twenty-three years old.

Because it makes me very sad to remember the bitter part of the story — which is forever final — I thought I might just avoid writing about Wayne. But how on earth could I do that? I loved him very much and he was a big part of my life for a long time. And if I don't talk about him, who will? He deserves his place at least in this story.

The record of Wayne's life before it joined ours is sketchy. He told us himself that he had been in many foster homes. He said that he must be a very bad boy to have been moved around so much: nobody wanted to keep him. What a terrible thing for a small child to feel! How often I tried to reassure him. A number of times he asked me, "Who do you think was my really mother?" I could not give him an answer, for all that the social worker told us was that he had probably never known his biological mother, that he was raised as an infant by his grandmother and that she was seen to be negligent enough that the Children's Aid Society stepped in.

Wayne, 12 years old

Although he had every reason to be disturbed, I don't think anyone would say that Wayne was a difficult child. We had our rough
times, but looking back, there were fewer of these than in many other
families we knew. Unfortunately, my husband didn't love Wayne
wholeheartedly. He and Wayne circled one another and never walked
hand-in-hand. Wayne didn't conform to his new father's idea of a good
little boy and so he was pretty well blocked from a father-son relationship. There could also have been jealousy on Robert's part of my close
relationship with Wayne and that would have added to his rejection
of the little lad. Robert would not agree that there was a problem and
wouldn't discuss his feelings toward Wayne.

When I first met this waif of a boy in my grade two classroom, he
could read especially well. He could read from the newspaper by the
time he came to be ours that first summer. It was a joy for me to listen
to him read and then to take my turn reading to him. We would make
up stories together and sometimes write them down. Quite lovely.

Wayne and I also shared a love of music. We would sit together
on the piano bench and as I played songs we would sing together. Even
as an eight year old, Wayne preferred to sing harmony parts rather than
the melody line — something I could never do. What great sessions we
had! Later, when he was in secondary school, Wayne decided that he
would like to learn to play the trumpet and to join the school band. He
would listen to records of Herb Alpert and blast away as best he could.
The dog would howl. His good ear was a help but also a hindrance: he
never learned to read music because as soon as he would hear a part,
he could play it and not attend to the charts. The band teacher, whom
I knew well socially and professionally, told me that Wayne was his
biggest disappointment; he learned to play the instrument so easily but
he just would not persevere with the reading. I find it interesting to
think of the way learning mathematics and learning to produce music
are said to be aligned and how Wayne did not master either one; mathematics defeated him all the way through school and he never learned
to read music.

I knew about his academic troubles, of course, but the extent of
his disability in mathematics was brought home to me even after he

completed secondary school. Wayne had bought a crumpled old car and one day he told me that he was trying to find out what mileage he was getting. I said, "Well, Wayne, just divide the number of miles you have driven by the amount of gas you have bought." He looked at me with some disgust and said, "Mother, don't you know that I never did learn to do division?"

Although quite small, Wayne was a fine athlete, quick and agile. When he was in grade ten, he was asked to join the senior basketball team, a significant honour. But Wayne had trouble sticking with things. When I asked him why he was not going to basketball practice he said, "Oh I think that team can get along very well without me," and I couldn't convince him to stay with it.

Somehow this inability to follow through on a commitment was always with him. But as it turned out, that didn't matter in the long run. What *did* matter to me, and what was sweet, were the golden moments we had together.

It is amazing how little vignettes from those years flash through my mind when I least expect them to. We ran one time through some glorious fall leaves in Campbell River Park. I often think of that scene. There had been a huge storm which had knocked down many trees, and the civic workers had piled and burned the smaller branches. The ground was still covered with layers and layers of leaves from the great maple trees that towered over the park. When we reached the park that afternoon, it was close to dusk and we ran about amongst the leaves, crunching them and tossing them as the light failed and the embers of the large fires still glowed. How my heart aches now each year when the leaves fall.

One summer when he was about eleven, Wayne set up a great messy conglomerate of radio wires and pieces of this and that to make a short-wave radio system. How was it that he could do this and yet never learn long-division? That holiday time, there was a great traipsing of young boys in and out of the house, looking very serious and purpose-ful, sending messages to one another and requiring rides to the store to get more wire or another set of earphones.

With the first car love affair, what terrible junkie vehicles scarred our back yard. The spasmodic beasts that sputtered and shot flames from one end or the other never did become roadworthy — vehicles of frustration, not propulsion. The hulk-renovating episodes were preceded by attempts to drive my almost-as-junkie Volkswagen. We had a circular driveway in our yard, a fine practice track for Wayne to use, shifting gears and steering his way, sometimes through the sacrificial flower beds. There was also a wonderful grassy pathway out through the trees. In the winter, the path was slippery and there were large puddles on either side. On one occasion, Wayne needed a couple of friends to get him out of the great mud hole in which the car was almost submerged.

We did have some royal battles. As I talk to other people whose kids grew up in the sixties and seventies, I am sure that our battles — "Time to get up. Get up! *Get up!*" and "How can your room be disinfected, let alone cleaned, with everything you own on the floor?" — were not much different than those in other families. Drugs and alcohol, the worst destroyers of youth in that era, were never a factor with Wayne. He said he liked to be in charge of himself.

Wayne taught me about waving people goodbye. He was going out in his car one time and said to me, "Mom, do you know how good it feels to have someone wave at you until you are out of sight?" Of course, I did that with him from then on. But I also do it with other people. Always. Guests leaving and seeing me outside waiting to wave them away will say, "Get inside, Beth. Don't stand out here in the rain." But I wait for them to go. And then I think of Wayne.

Wayne dropped out of school halfway through grade twelve after sabotaging his year by spending his time in the local pool hall. I had not known about the pool hall and have accused myself of not paying attention. The following year he did go back and finish secondary school. In the meantime, he worked for a farm auctioneer whose barns were a mile or so away from where we lived. The job was to clean the barns — "my regular shit-shovelling job," Wayne called it. This kind of work seemed a good way for him to learn the merits of an education. After graduation, he trained to become a realtor. Achieving success at selling houses in the area where we lived was beyond him, so he bought a trailer to live in and pulled it up to Penticton, 300 miles away. After two or three months, we drove up to see him and decided that his living conditions were all right.

In October that year there was a teachers' convention in Penticton to which I drove with a couple of other teachers. I took Wayne out for dinner that evening and afterwards he wanted me to go with him to the dance hall that he frequented with his new friends. He was adamant that I should dance with him. Later, he said, "Now look, Mother. How many guys my age would want to take their mother to dance with them in the place where his friends hang out?" I was proud.

It was the last time I ever saw Wayne. One cold night soon after, he had been skating with friends, returned to his trailer, lit the furnace but failed to open a window. He fell asleep and never woke up.

The Piano

From before we left the Magritchy place at Moose Jaw until the year I helped Orpha at her school, I had taken piano lessons. Mother found a piano teacher for the three of us; Sadie was probably about twenty-five years old and seemed to be cloistered, living with her parents who were the wealthiest farmers in the neighbourhood. Their house was large and always seemed cold, as did Sadie and her mother. Sadie's piano existed all by itself in a small room toward the back of the house. It was smaller than ours and shiny with white keys that were really white, not yellowish like ours. Sadie taught us middle C and four notes on either side and we practised our lessons every day. But in only a few weeks we moved away from Moose Jaw and the piano lessons stopped for some time.

I was thought to have musical talent and so my lessons resumed despite my parents' scarce resources. After we moved to the Forestry Farm, I began taking piano lessons again, now from a woman who was one of the most respected piano teachers in Saskatoon. For several years I took the bus into the city once a week, never really overcoming my timidity of the great studio with its four grand pianos and its rarefied artistic atmosphere that dared me to drop a book or close a door too loudly. Although vastly different in their location, the teaching pianos that I experienced seemed to be approached almost reverently and always solemnly. This teacher was tall, dressed very carefully but always in one of the same two outfits for a whole year. She seldom

Beth accompanies The Surrey Singers

smiled, although she never reproved me either. Together we worked through the Toronto Conservatory of Music system, the Canadian gold standard for classical music education at the time.

When I was in Book VII and about eleven years old, my teacher asked me to enter a festival that some of the teachers in the city had organized for their pupils. I think everyone was surprised when I won. I certainly was. Mother got a new dress for me to wear to the presentation event and Father, in his Sunday best, drove me to the studio. When we arrived, my teacher, with great embarrassment, explained that the presentation was to be made to the teacher, not the pupil. Father and I trundled off home again.

As I grew up, I realized that I had neither a good "ear" for music nor did I memorize well, so I did not aspire to be a soloist. But I was often told that I had a "lovely touch," and I could read music easily — two qualities needed by a good accompanist. I liked to do that and was often asked to play the piano for a choir or a soloist to practise or perform. Once when I accompanied a children's choir at a festival in Vancouver, the adjudicator singled me out and said to the audience, "Every choir leader should have a pianist like this lady." What wonderful encouragement for continuing in my avocation. Piano-playing became an important part of my life, opening doors for me and introducing me to new people and new situations.

Music camp was one of these situations. The camp, held near the end of August each year, was organized by its music director to be a "warm-up" for the students in the band and choir programs of a secondary school near where we lived. One year the regular choir accompanist became ill at camp time and suggested that I replace her, which I did. What a great time that was! I had joined a team comprising teachers, several parents and a nurse to support the music program — an assignment that we happily accepted for several years in a row. Bivouacked at the edge of a nearby lake, the group engaged in many activities as well as music practice — water sports, swimming, canoeing and water-skiing — all directed by a physical education teacher from the school. A social director planned campfire parties for the whole crowd and the adults discussed educational theories far into the night. I made lifelong friends at music camp, not only with some of the adults but with some of the students as well. There seemed to be a particularly trusting and appreciative atmosphere at these camps for which I give the director the credit. I became aware of the way the group's behaviour was affected by the behaviour of the leader. His appreciation of every person there affected the attitudes of all of us toward him and toward everyone else. This was a lesson that was repeated for me a few years later and that stood me in good stead when I was placed in a leadership position myself.

As well as accompanying this school choir and others, I played the organ in a variety of churches. After I had learned to play my grandfather's pump organ when Father sacrificed Avery to the war effort, there were a number of occasions when I was asked to help to provide music in a church, using a similar organ. Not many books of music were available at that time, so almost everything I played was straight out of the old black "hymnary." My remembrance of that music is of a continual sort of middle-C drone.

After we had settled in Tudor and my teaching was going along successfully, I began many long years playing the organ in Cloverdale United Church. I abandoned it for a while when I found it too difficult to reconcile my lack of faith in prescribed church doctrine with my dedication to leading the church music. In time, though, I decided that no one was asking, or probably caring very much, about what I believed and that I didn't need to concern myself about the insincerity of my presentation: my thoughts were my own and it was only the music that I was providing.

The culmination of the organ playing occurred at a concert in a large church in New Westminster when I played a Casavant, one of the great Canadian-built organs of our day, to accompany several combined choirs under the direction of the head of music at the city college. How I worked to prepare for that concert! A friend helped me to master some of the intricacies of this particular organ model, everything from how to turn it on to how to make it speak in several voices. For a while I thought "The King of Instruments," as it is sometimes called, would defeat me. When the choirs gathered for the one and only rehearsal, I had not learned to quiet its roar: the too robust accompaniment was unacceptable. More practice. More practice. In the end, it was a grand concert and, during the social hour that followed, the intimidating master-director offered me a job teaching at his college. I didn't take it as a real offer, and didn't consider taking him up on it; I'm sure he never intended me to. But what a feeling of accomplishment for the little girl who once squirmed on the bench during her piano lessons near Moose Jaw. What a bullet in the *Something to Do* arsenal.

Belle

Belle was a buckskin quarter horse. She was creamy coloured with a flowing black mane and tail. Quarter horses are popular in western Canada where they are valued as ranch horses for their ability to sprint short distances and where they star in calf roping and barrel racing events. They are also trained as show horses where they must follow directions to walk, lope, jog, sidestep, back up and stop.

I bought Belle from a neighbour whose daughter had tired of riding her pretty horse around their two-acre property. Robert and I had seen an ad in the local paper that said, "Quarter Horse for sale, 15 hands, $450." Just what I was looking for. We went to see how she looked and in no time I was riding her around the neighbour's paddock. Three of my friends came along to watch this private rodeo, terrified that it would be more than I could handle. Belle was prancy, but she neither bounced me off nor refused to move. We seemed to get along well. A local veterinarian that we hired to look her over said we couldn't go wrong by buying that little mare, so we did that and arranged to have her brought to our property. We had prepared a small paddock and modified an old chicken house to serve as a one-horse barn. We were almost recklessly confident that all of this would work, for we had also prepared a sawdust ring around a grassy acre at the back of the property.

Now why would a middle-aged primary school teacher who had always considered herself to be an athletic moron, and had usually been rather frightened of animals, want to own a quarter horse? As a ranch horse? As a show horse? Not possible. What then?

I was bored. I was probably at the top of my game as a teacher. I knew about changing my teaching style and my teaching assignments to stave off boredom, but that wasn't enough. I was looking for a completely different kind of stimulation. The idea of having a horse came from watching a friend as she exercised her beautiful animal. I was entranced. She told me that a horse, particularly a pretty animal with a lively spirit, is a lovely pet. She said that, not only riding it, but watching it skip around a field, feeling it nuzzle you with its warm nose, being surprised each time it runs toward you when you bring oats — all are part of the joy of it.

Of course, I had known horses as a child on the farms at Moose Jaw and Caron, but that was entirely different. Entirely. Those farm animals were designed for work, big plodding creatures that didn't encourage me to get close. No pets, these. Best beware of the heavy feet and avoid the lustreless, accusing eyes. One of them, Jesse, pulled the buggy in which we were taken to school. Being transported by Jesse didn't present a pretty picture from our point of view. We would sit just behind the buckboard of the buggy, very close to Jesse's rear end. That's what we could see of her all along the three and a half miles to and from the school. Her large flaccid haunches moved steadily up and down in front of us. Every now and then she would lift her tail and let fall a great plop of manure. The ass hole would close again to look like a dried fig, below which we would see a great chain of fleshy parts that looked ugly and unnecessary. "What is all that below Jesse's hole, Mother?" "Never mind. Hold the reins for a minute please, while I straighten this seat."

Belle, on the other hand, was neat. She had full rounded haunches and a neat rear end. I was proud of the way her compact body moved so gracefully and quickly.

When I told Father about Belle, he had no patience with the idea at all. For him, a horse was a means of transportation only used when that was the best one could do; the thought of a horse as a pet was not part of his lexicon. He did not appreciate how riding Belle brought me wonderful hours of pleasure, sensuous and exhilarating. Getting her to walk, to canter, to gallop, feeling her warmth under me, sensing the wind in my hair — all a marvellous free feeling.

At one point I took a bad fall. It was my own fault: Belle and I had been racing a bit with a pony in the neighbouring field; I dropped a rein and, unable to control Belle, decided to kick my boots free of the stirrups and fall off before we both went through the fence. I landed on hard ground. I knew that I had hurt myself, but since I was alone I had to stump across the ring to where Belle was standing contritely, mount her and ride her in to the paddock. It was a long time before I could ride her again, for my ankle was broken and I had to wear a cast for several weeks.

That August, still wearing the cast, I started a new job at Simon Fraser University. One of the other new staff members told me that appearing in a cast gave me a certain cachet — everyone asking how I had broken my ankle and by my answer, that I had fallen off my horse, presenting myself to our new colleagues as a sporting little horse-woman.

I suppose I enjoyed the image. In fact, I know I did. Maybe that is why I wanted a horse in the first place: I wanted to be a sporting little lady of forty-two years.

In another three years I had a change of work assignment and, because of that, I don't think I was ever bored again. I sold Belle to a school principal who was delighted with how well she performed in gymkhana events. How she had marked time with me! It had never entered my head to try barrel racing.

For those three years, Belle provided for me the *Something to Look Forward To* element of happiness: I looked forward every day to the time I would spend with her.

A Bit of Principaling

Wayne was our only child. Although I wanted to conceive I did not and in time decided that since I was not going to bear a child, and that looking after Tudor was hardly fulfilling, I would set about becoming the best teacher I could possibly be. I worked at becoming a specialist in the field of primary education, finishing undergraduate degrees in arts and education, acquiring experience in several public schools and attending conferences whenever I could find an appropriate one.

I was teaching in a primary classroom in a medium-sized school in one of the poor socio-economic regions of the Surrey school district, when unexpectedly I became a school administrator. It happened because the principal of the school where I was teaching became ill and was absent for two or three months. His absence was particularly unfortunate because of the circumstances surrounding a certain teacher in the school. This person was not only inexperienced as a teacher, but was also inhibited because he was a new Canadian with poor English language skills. He was unable to prevent some of the older children from commandeering his classroom. Inevitably, the ensuing chaos spilled out into the rest of the school. The staff was worried about the situation and so convened a strategizing session. The decision was made to delegate two experienced teachers to meet with the superintendent, apprise him of the situation and solicit some help. I was one of those experienced teachers. When my colleague and I phoned the school board office to explain our dilemma, the superintendent, Jack Evans, came to our school at once and the two of us presented our account of the staff's concerns.

I suspect that the upper administrative staff had already deliberated about the situation at our school, but even if so, neither of us knew that. After he had listened to us for a few minutes, Mr. Evans said, "Right. I am going to appoint an interim principal — the most experienced and best qualified teacher on the staff. That will be you, Beth."

My reaction was not elegant. "That doesn't make sense," I said. "What you need is a strong young man." Shame. I did say that. He sat and looked at me and waited and waited. I could see my colleague, out of the superintendent's line of vision, mouthing to me, "Do it. Do it." I folded. I agreed to take on the job and off went the superintendent to the various classrooms to tell the teachers that I was the acting principal.

I went into the uninhabited principal's office, closed the door and stood in front of the window. I said to myself, "Now think. Think. It is not a strong young man that is needed: it is wisdom. Think." So I settled down and thought. I thought about what would be the first, most important thing for me to do. I decided that most of all I needed the confidence and cooperation of the staff, for I certainly would not be able to succeed without them. I called the teachers to meet with me after school, asked them for their confidence and support, and we agreed that together we could make the school function well again.

There followed a heady time — heady because of the learning, the growing, the call for leadership, the acceptance of responsibility. It was almost like salad days again.

The superintendent, on his slalom around the school on my inaugural day as principal, had seen at once that the situation in the rampant classroom could not be redeemed by the teacher who was there, so the very next day he reappeared at the school to suspend the teacher. As he left he said, "Now it is up to you, Beth, to find another teacher." Well. There was a list of applicants at the school board office from which I could make a start. I realized that I needed to take into account the culture of the school and the immediate needs of the students and the teachers. I had started this enterprise with the conviction that it had to be a cooperative project, so I asked a staff member to interview three people with me. We chose an inexperienced but confident young man. We told him that this class had run amok and that we had chosen him to set it right because he appeared to be someone who would be able to gain the trust and respect of the students. He did that. Very soon there was peace in the hallways and learning in the classrooms.

Because I was a novice and a keener, I was easily persuaded to charge the ramparts for this or that cause. And because I was new and eager, I was blessed, not damned, for my sometimes inept attempts to get help. One cause, for instance, was to secure more library books. I knew that the real principal was aware of the lack of books, but I was an innocent on the loose and took advantage of it. I approached the rather formidable chief librarian who admitted to having some discretionary funds that she would use for us. Before long, a big new shipment of library books was delivered to the school.

This was my honeymoon period as a principal. Because I was an acolyte, I possessed a certain boldness that became a habit. I do not believe that my further development in a leadership role was enhanced by the "professional development" sessions that were presented to school administrators at that time. We seemed to be *warned* rather than *inspired*, told to step carefully rather than boldly, encouraged to follow protocol rather than to show initiative. I thought what was required of leaders was the courage that Hemingway called "grace under pressure." When I remember the stupid things that I did and the way they were forgiven, set right or forgotten, I only wish I had been even bolder.

Help sometimes emerged from unexpected corners. A teacher I hardly knew approached me out of the blue to say that she had admired as a principal a certain man whom I had seen on various occasions — an urbane, quiet-spoken gentleman. She said that when this man was her principal, his manner had been so gentle, so polite, so thoughtful, his whole behaviour so exemplary, that all of the members of the staff were better behaved than they had been at any other time. It was similar to the saying, "Everyone plays better hockey when they play with Wayne Gretzky." I was reminded of the music camp director and the effect he had upon the people in his charge. What great advice from a teacher, advice given in a subtle and kindly way. Although I never knew him well, that gentleman administrator became my leader-ship model.

After two months of this exhilarating experience as leader, the real principal recovered his health and returned to be in charge; I returned to the classroom. "It's a good thing that I like you," I said to him, "or I would have hated to see you return. I really liked your job." I was most grateful to have experienced a bit of school administration, to have survived it with my reputation as an educator intact and to have gained new confidence in my leadership potential.

Before that school year ended I was thrilled to be appointed as head teacher of a beautiful new school, Jessie Lee, that was still being built.

A Real Principal

Before Jessie Lee opened, I had been instructed to call a meeting of the people in the surrounding community and to tell them my philosophy of education. I winced at the assignment, for it seemed to me that more wisdom and knowledge was being required of me than I possessed. There could be no retreat. How I laboured to prepare a statement that was honest, that was politically acceptable, that displayed excitement about the new project that lay before us all.

On the day of the meeting I went to the beauty parlour to have my hair primped and while I was watching the procedure in the mirror, I suddenly felt very, very warm and I saw that my face had flushed to a deep red, right down to the top of my dress. "Good heavens," I thought, "I'm having a hot flush. What timing! What unbelievably bad timing." I dared not revert to the ugly feeling of the little girl from Saskatchewan; I could only grab for the stoicism of my prairie roots.

About a hundred people came to the meeting, more than I had expected. As I was making my presentation, an elderly gentleman interrupted me and questioned me at least three times. I felt myself teetering on the podium but I hung on and managed to keep my balance. Later, I was reassured to hear that this person made a habit of challenging speakers, whatever their subject. He probably did me a favour by keeping me alert and steadfast in my philosophical stance.

It seems strange now to reflect upon the extent of the responsibility and incumbent freedom that I was given, the most important of which was to be charged with the selection of the staff — a marvellous opportunity to build a cohesive team that could initiate the development of a new school. Together we clarified our mission and set out our expectations for ourselves, for the children and for the parents. A few watchers said that ours was to be a "free school." I didn't like that. In those days, a free school connoted a school without rules, with unrestricted licence for any kind of behaviour, without assurance of the great joy of learning. What we intended was to create a school where children were *free to learn*.

As a school community, we were oblivious to the need to get approval for a number of matters concerning the use of the school building and grounds; we just moved on blithely as if the school were our home. Again, it is hard to believe that there was a time when standardization and uniformity were not the order of the day and when creativity and originality were lauded, not stifled under careful surveillance. At that time, our society seemed to be a less litigious one, less frightening and inhibiting for innovators. Conformity did not dull the colours of schools. Ours glowed with its creativity and attracted visitors from around the province.

Not everything we tried was accepted without question, of course. It was a new experience for me to have a parent complain about a teacher's action — and to find myself held responsible. One time a parent phoned to say, "What's going on here? At your school a teacher is *asking* students to bring *knives* to school." The teacher, Sue Hammel, had indeed done so — because the small kitchen knives were to be used for a certain art project using clay. Sue did not see any reason for any complaint nor to warn me that there could be one: she had not anticipated that these knives could be seen as menacing in any way. "Tell her to keep her knives at home if she wants to," was the teacher's reply. "But she needs to understand the difference between a weapon and a tool." After I explained the project to the parent, she decided not to worry about the innocuous tools that her child and the others brought to school the next day. These were halcyon times.

As the children arrived each day, many of them driven to school by their parents, I would stand outside the entrance door to meet them.

I had not seen this happen in other schools, but it seemed a natural practice for our special place. So too were the weekly pupil tea parties in the principal's office.

Except for a few anomalies, I found that the skills that I needed as a teacher in order to work effectively with children were the same skills that I needed as a principal to work effectively with teachers and parents. I reminded myself about the principles that my teacher-mentor had told our class long ago: that we must never allow ourselves to dislike a student and that we must never seek to make ourselves irreplaceable. It was a little harder for me to comply with the first maxim when I was dealing with adults than when I was working with children, perhaps because teachers and parents were in a position to threaten my authority — which was pretty tenuous, particularly at first. I remembered the behaviour of the music director and the urbane administrator who set the tone for those with whom they worked, and I worked hard at emulating them.

I had been appointed as head teacher, not principal, of this new school. It was too small to have its own principal and so was attached to another elementary school with a principal who headed them both. Although theoretically I reported to that principal, he had in fact been told to leave us to our own devices — which he did. That fall, I heard rumours that things were not working well with him at the other school and that he might be replaced. The thought of such a change filled me with anxiety lest a new man would compromise our independence. In November, this principal did break down. I was astounded to be informed that I was to be his replacement, to become acting principal of the two schools Jessie Lee and H.T. Thrift.

This promotion came at a very bad time for me: Wayne died on the very day that the principal had to be replaced. Stunned with grief, I did not pay much attention to what had happened concerning the administration of the school.

A certain numbness was all I felt. I was numb to criticisms of my appointment — for there were administrators and teachers who felt I wasn't prepared for what was now a significant position — and numb to the weight of worry about what I needed to accomplish. Numb also to the comfort offered by my friends and relatives.

Work was therapy and there was enough of it to do. I had unexpectedly become principal of two schools; I had given birth to the first of these and had adopted the second. The adopted school presented more challenges and conditions, which could result in more mistakes, than did the newborn one. At the first school we pranced along; at the second we stumbled through.

One particular mistake haunted me. More than that, it humbled me. I was critical of a particular teacher (justifiably so) but even though I had been warned about criticizing teachers, that this was an era when even experienced principals had been brought down or at least made to look like fools for careless criticisms, still I blazed away feeling bold and righteous. The blunder I made was to write a note to this teacher suggesting that he was not adequately meeting his students' needs, and to copy that note to his supervisor. Stupid. That is just not done. The teacher was angry enough to get in touch with the teachers' union, which readily demanded that I write an apology to their member. I confessed my crime to my mentor, the superintendent, who said in a fatherly way, "What did you do a stupid thing like that for?" and told me to comply with the demand immediately. I did that, of course, and fortunately for me, nothing more came of it. Well, almost nothing.

I soon realized that news of my foolhardiness had gone beyond the school when, out of the blue, one of my friends, a teacher at a neighbouring school, told me about this wonderful teacher in my adopted school, naming the very person with whom I had been in conflict. She told me that he was a beautiful person and an exceptional teacher. Why was I suddenly given this information just after my major stumble over this very person, someone who had never been mentioned to me before?

Clearly, blunders resounded. But happily, some bells rang, too. My years of experience as a classroom teacher had provided me with in-depth knowledge of the curriculum and the materials supporting it. I was not just the oldest but also the most experienced of any staff member in either school, and I had also been an inveterate attendee at conferences and in-service settings. Having been seconded for one year to Simon Fraser University to help with the training and supervision of student teachers, I had been exposed to many styles of teaching and had been given an opportunity to interact professionally with a number of colleagues. As a school principal, I was now able to extend my experience from the boundaries of a classroom to the parameters of whole schools. This opportunity was a privilege and a delight for me. For instance, when a member of the staff asked me to recommend a supplementary text to help her reach certain children in her class, I knew at once just what was needed. It pleased me to be able to capitalize on my experience. Sometimes I felt a sense of freedom as if I had burst out of the confines of the classroom and into the welcome expanse of the school.

The two schools had quite different cultures. Almost as soon as it opened, the brand new school could go along very well without me. The staff members had been chosen to constitute a team and to have supportive strengths. As a result, decisions were often made by the group of them and my role was to be an expeditor and supporter. In my view, this was an ideal situation.

The adopted school comprised teachers with many strengths, but there were some fractures in their relationships. Minor management matters caused rifts — the state of the staffroom sink, for instance, was a constant irritant to a few people who posted a sign saying, "Your mother isn't looking after you here," and there was trouble over the schedule for using the gymnasium. This kind of bickering stopped when team spirit emerged as the stronger staff members were encouraged to assert themselves. Social leaders stepped forward to arrange dinners and parties that helped us to bond with one another. Much of this staff worked as a unit for a number of years after I moved on.

As soon as I became a school principal, I enrolled in a master's program in educational administration. I believe the master's study program itself was of limited significance in leadership or administration growth, but the contact it facilitated with other people in the field was invaluable and to be studying the theory of school administration at the same time as I was actually immersed in the practice was a grand experience. For two years, I attended one class during the winter months and two during the summer months. I was quite sorry when the program was completed.

At the end of my first year as principal of the two schools, I was required to apply for the principal's position, the position I had been filling as an interim leader. Along with two other candidates, both men, I was short-listed and interviewed by school board members. By now, though, the tables had turned: the superintendent had introduced women to the field of school administration and the trustees had followed his lead. When the three of us were told that I had been the successful candidate, one of the men said to me, "You might say that you were in the best position. You are a woman." Damn. I thought I was the best candidate.

Challenging Times

After three years — exciting and fulfilling years — I was offered a transfer to the principalship of L.A. Matheson Junior Secondary School. I immediately drove round to reconnoitre, to make an initial assessment of the situation.

The heavy entrance door stuck a bit when I first opened it. "Not a very welcoming entrance," I thought. "Is this symbolic of a sticky situation that I may be getting into? Don't be silly. The door just needs a little maintenance work." Once inside, a wide hallway stretched away ahead almost as far as I could see. I walked on down this passage between the lockers marshalled like soldiers in close ranks on both sides of a compound. Some soldiers were bashed about a little, all securely locked, their uniforms battleship grey, unadorned except for the lock insignia.

I nosed into an empty classroom. How very different from the elementary school classrooms that I knew so well, where the walls were showcases for student art that marked all of the seasons and the special days — gaily coloured leaves in the fall, pumpkins and witches for Halloween, paper snowflakes and coloured chains in December. How sterile this junior secondary classroom looked to me. What a contrast to the over-the-top liveliness of the elementary school classrooms.

I found the office and looked in across the counter that separated the ins and the outs. The office looked like a huge paper bin. Five large filing cabinets were stacked with paper and six desks were distressed with scattered sheets. A great duplicating machine worked frantically to spit out dozens of copies per minute. The paper piles grew as I watched. There was no one in sight.

In a few minutes, a loud bell rang interminably and hundreds of students filled the hallway. I stood aside and observed. Some of the students assaulted the lockers, some huddled together in groups of three or four, some hurried toward an open classroom door. A number of turban-headed youths sped along, staying close to the outside edge of the hall, hugging the stalwart lockers. Teachers walked by briskly going about the business of getting to their next station or bound for the office with a sheaf of papers — more paper.

I was filled with awe at the thought of immersion into this chaos. I hurried home to my orderly house, sat very still and said to myself, "Now think. Think." I remembered saying the same words to myself about three years earlier. Again, I realized that I would need the cooperation and support of the staff. A good way to start was offered to me within a few days: I was invited to a staff meeting to meet the teachers. I decided that all I could hope to do in this situation was to learn each person's name, but that would be a start at relationship building. I asked the senior secretary to send me a list of the teachers, organized according to their subject areas. She appreciated what I wanted to do and so one relationship had already begun — with the manager of the paper office, the lovely Helena Hiltz. At the staff meeting, the principal helped me by calling the teachers by name as they participated in the hour-long session. By the time we went to lunch after the meeting, I was able to go about the room, calling each person by name.

Now that I had met the staff, the aura of the school seemed to change. The teachers sparkled with their dedication to the students and pride in their work. Their dedication, not the initial unfriendly impression, defined the school for me.

My second visit to the school was to attend a band concert. In a most unexpected way, that did not go well. The car I was driving at the time was a Camaro. I whipped it into the parking lot behind the school and drove right up to the grassy strip at the edge of the field — just a little too far, as I quickly discovered: the heavy front end of the beast dipped down into a wide rut that held the front wheels as if they were in a vice. The Camaro wouldn't move. Help. Well, not right then: the concert was about to begin. I sat through two hours of the discordant squeaks and squawks that emerge from clarinets and trumpets in a young band, trying to smile and nod to anyone who looked my way, all the time writhing inside about how to get that cursed vehicle out of the ditch.

Of course I couldn't do it myself and had to get help from the three male teachers who waited around after the concert to shake my hand. I had learned that you do not need to be a strong young man to be a school administrator. In fact, I had long before resolved to always wear skirts and high heels. Did I really have to get into a situation like this that made me look like a dependent weakling? Well, the help was quickly and generously given. How lovely it was to learn a year or so later that the three men had made a pact not to tell anyone on the staff about my embarrassing predicament that evening. How good-hearted they were — and how unimportant was that goof!

Educators considered junior secondary schools to be the "pressure cookers" of the school system. The students were fourteen to sixteen years old, an age when they were questioning authority yet often not ready to accept responsibility. Some of the younger students needed help to make the transition from smaller, more intimate elementary schools to the larger, sometimes threatening junior secondary school. But it was a stretch for the oldest students, still adolescents themselves, to be strong enough role models for the younger ones. Eventually, district administrators and school boards realized that the junior secondary school division was not successful and it was phased out in the Surrey school district, replaced by the organization of schools that take students all the way from age fourteen to secondary school graduation. It has proven to be a much better plan.

In the meantime, though, I was one of the junior secondary school principals. I had accepted the appointment, trusting that three years of leadership in an elementary school were preparation enough to take on the pressures inherent in a junior secondary school. In fact, the positions were very different and I struggled to meet situations for which I was ill-prepared. I felt a bit of additional pressure to make a success of it, knowing that I was the only female principal of a secondary school in the province. Others, women in particular, wanted an example set that would help to improve the image of women and promote their status. And the school system wanted to demonstrate that women are as capable as men in such positions of responsibility.

Just as my perception of the school had changed dramatically when I met the teachers, so it was altered again when the classrooms were filled with students. For all that is said about the difficulties of getting along with youth during their years of puberty, it must also be said that during these years they are never boring.

The most rebellious times for secondary and post-secondary students were now behind us; school walk-outs when a whole student body would refuse to come into the building were a convulsion of the past. Now the disruption came from bomb threats. A secretary would receive a telephone call that a bomb would be detonated within perhaps fifteen minutes. Should the school be emptied just in case the threat was real? How should the principal react to what was probably a trick from a recalcitrant student? It was not as unnerving a situation as it sounds, for often the voice was recognized and the call traced to a dissident student now out of school. But it was an event that caused some anxious moments for the principal who had to call the shots.

Almost ten percent of the students in this school were first generation Canadians, their parents recent immigrants from India. For the most part, these students were steady and hard-working, but they were not well-integrated with the other students. After dismissal, confrontations between groups frequently occurred at the crossroads just two blocks from the school. No one was ever physically injured at that time — it was a cold war — but some feelings would be hurt and some students would be frightened. A number of the new Canadian parents, always the men, would come to my office to discuss possible solutions to the racial problems. Members of the delegation would appear in their own colourful country dress. I had great respect for their tenacity but did not find a ready answer to the problems.

At first it seemed to me that too many people got in the way of my direct involvement with the students. In the elementary schools, there had been only the teachers, not even a vice-principal, to come between me and the children — the people to whom the whole enterprise was directed. But now there was a vice-principal, counsellors, department heads and special needs teachers — all very necessary, but all increasing my remoteness from the students. I tried to be in the hallways when the classes changed, but that was a quite impersonal contact with these young people. In time it became clear to me that working directly with the students was not my essential role. I was meant to be a manager and a leader, not a teacher or a counsellor.

Neither was it my role to be the curriculum leader. As an elementary school principal, my knowledge of the curriculum had helped to make me feel secure and to give me credibility within the school community. In the secondary school, I did not have this knowledge. But this was not my role. It was my job to help to improve instruction and learning in the school through working with teachers — inspiring, encouraging and supporting them in their work with the students.

I attended workshops and read tirelessly about the supervision of instruction. From the distillation of those studies, my most significant conviction was that all of us grow from strength and that the most help I could offer to anyone was to identify their strengths so that they could improve their instructional methods through applying those strengths to their work. This conviction became one of the most important tenets of my leadership style.

While I was in the second of my three years at the junior secondary school, the superintendent decreed that all of the junior secondary schools should be evaluated. Sam McDowell, the lead superintendent for L.A. Matheson, informed the staff members — in my presence — that *they* were not being evaluated; it was the principal who was being appraised. He then told me privately that he knew I could stand up to the perceived threat and that his intention had been to put the teachers at ease. *They* told me privately that they would make sure that I got a good report. With their help, I did.

Nevertheless, despite the encouraging report I had received, I concluded that my contribution to the school was not outstanding and the stress of this principalship enormous. When I had accepted the transfer from the elementary school to the junior secondary, I had not understood how different the jobs were. Without experience in leadership or administration at this level, I was not prepared for the particular problems that I would encounter. I never knew what might be thrown at me next. The early teen years, for instance, present unique difficulties for many parents and teachers, and although my prime role was not with the students they were ultimately my responsibility. Distraught parents or teachers looked to me for magical ways to deal with recalcitrant or failing students. Then, the performance of some teachers was just not satisfactory so, despite my practice of helping people to grow from strength, there were those who simply did not succeed and needed to be discontinued as teachers, at least at this level. Again, this was my responsibility.

I remembered a sermon from long ago when the congregation was told, "Don't talk about your external pressure; talk about your internal fortitude." Well, my internal fortitude was wearing thin. Good evidence of that was the war I had to declare again on the fat factor; I had gained some weight. I took a good look at my status with regard to the happiness formula. Clearly I wasn't doing very well: the *Something to Do* was not providing a sense of achievement. It was my responsibility to take care of that. Before the end of the third year at the junior secondary school, I began to look for another job. I had started this assignment feeling perky and poised; I left it feeling tired and troubled.

Much more troubling was the end of my marriage to Robert. I do not talk about that marriage now: recriminations or accusations with regard to Robert or me would be neither pleasant to dwell upon nor to read. But apparently the *Someone to Love* component was not in good shape either.

Living Alone

I stood in front of the mirror in the bathroom to set in place my most expensive earrings. One slipped from my fingers and down the drain it went. Now what? I knew about *the trap*, the ugly curved pipe that was usually hidden in the cupboard under the sink. I had always avoided any acquaintance with it but now, ready or not, I would have to meet it face to face. I did not approach the trap unarmed, though, for a friend had provided me with a list of must-have tools that I had dutifully collected and stored with other emergency supplies. One of the tools was a monkey wrench, its great jaws yearning to circle the pipe that held the trap. The trap flashed hard looks at the wrench, but capitulated surprisingly quickly. I was astounded to find that I could disconnect the trap, find the precious earring in the ugly guck, replace the now blessed trap, turn on the water — and *there was no leak*. I telephoned almost every person I knew, hollering, "Listen to what I've done … I'd certainly rather not live alone, but if I can do this, I can survive." And survive I did, in my little seaside home in White Rock.

Not everything worked that well. For instance, I decided to add an extension to my little house in order to accommodate an indoor hot tub on one floor and an office in a room underneath. Almost immediately, the hot tub connection leaked and water from the tub found its way down to the office, frying the computer printer and sogging my papers and books. Messy, costly and beyond monkey-wrenching. Also costly was another malfunction: the contractor skipped town before he finished the building project. So I made the acquaintance of a good plumber and a nice lawyer (though not as nice a one as I met some years later).

I decided to do without a lawyer on my next project. After a two-year separation, it appeared to be a good idea to divorce Robert, but I didn't want to talk to anybody about our relationship. Since Robert and I had no disputes about property or family, the process was not likely to be complicated, so what need did I have for a lawyer? The local pharmacy had a divorce how-to kit that gave detailed instructions (about a hundred of them!) that, taken one at a time, were not insurmountable. The first task, for instance, was to provide a copy of my birth certificate. "Now what does that have to do with it?" I grumbled to myself, but just found it and proceeded to item two.

The finale was the court appearance. My friend Rose came along to help me quiver through that experience, which did not prove to be the bogy that I had imagined. I had thought that all judges were stern, remote creatures, but this one was no such thing. He looked at me in a kindly, almost fatherly, way. Afterwards Rose took me to tea (tea!) where a fortune teller read our cups. This soothsayer told Rose that she had a lovely, soft personality that would entice many people to love her; she told me that I was flinty and forbidding and that I would do well to ease off. I decided that she was a charlatan.

Traveling alone was rather fun. True, the lack of a companion to share experiences with was a drag, but you do make more effort to become acquainted with other people when you travel alone. For instance, when I went on a tour of Spain, Portugal and North Africa, there was a school principal who seemed quite charming. I soon discovered that he was already with a traveling companion; when he manoeuvred me to a space beside the Goya exhibition in the Prado and asked me to meet him after the tour, I decided he was a bit of a bastard. I'm sure he thought I was flinty.

No such encounter in Japan where I traveled from Tokyo to Nagasaki by train, stopping at cities along the way. The language problem was profound, probably mostly because I was determined to inhabit Japanese-style inns and not glitzy North American hotels. I would find inns that provided full board so I did not have to order from an unfathomable menu. Good decision. For each meal, I would be brought a huge array of small bowls and would work my way through each one. I wrote to friends about the six-bowl or nine-bowl meals. One time a bowl contained soft cooked eggs — a challenge to eat with chopsticks and a time when being served privately in my room was an etiquette advantage.

A safari to the game parks in Kenya was the most exciting traveling I had ever done. This was no trip between luxury resorts, but a pitch-your-own-tent, wash-in-a-basin, bring-your-sleeping-bag event, arranged by adventurous friends. Sleeping in a small tent with a Masai warrior leaning on his rifle by an all-night fire, I felt close to the animals but never frightened of them. At that time, Nairobi was a beautiful cosmopolitan city and in the countryside there did not appear to be any of the poverty with which I would become very well acquainted some years later. I came home from the safari with stars in my eyes and a set of photos to be treasured.

Mother enjoyed looking at my photos more than anyone else. By now she and I had changed roles: I was the supporter as Mother's life drifted away. Death did not pounce on her as it had on Wayne and later on Father. A mishandled prostate operation had put an untimely, unexpected end to Father's life. Without him by her side, Mother was stalwart until she began to crumble both physically and mentally. The greatest difficulty for me did not come with her death, but with watching her decline, becoming a victim of bullies who took away her power. When she finally gave up struggling with death — with which she certainly did struggle — I felt we were both relieved.

I learned that it is easy to feel like a victim when living alone: a victim of circumstances, of a person, of an unfair world. I admit to succumbing to a few day-long pouts when I felt that life was unkind and unfair, but most of the time I revelled in my freedom from the constraints that shared living can impel. I lived alone for eleven years — years that I enjoyed most of the time.

The Best Career Years

When I began to look for another job, to my delight a supervisor's job became available in my own school district. I was encouraged to apply to join the central office staff as supervisor of the arts, and acquired this position. It pleased me to be assigned to a *staff* position, which meant that I did not make reports on those that I supervised, rather than a *line* position, where reporting to and from were mandatory. Because supervisors did not write reports, we were in a good position to support and encourage teachers and principals without intimidating them. Unfortunately, staff positions have since gone out of style with increasingly straight lines of authority. I believe that move is in exactly the wrong direction — in the education system, we should be working toward the elimination, or at least the reduction, of hierarchies — but nobody important listened to me.

Two years after I began my lovely new job, hard times descended on the province and the education system was dealt punishing blows: class sizes increased, programs and positions were cut, and retiring supervisors were not replaced. My job was greatly expanded in order to fill some of the gaps. I became supervisor of secondary education, with responsibilities for programs and instruction for all of the required secondary-level courses: English, social studies, science and mathematics.

My most significant contribution as a supervisor of secondary instruction was to instigate and help to arrange professional development for teachers. This was a drought area, particularly in the secondary sector where facilitating gatherings to fertilize teacher growth was welcomed by many teachers. It was fun and it was productive. Work in some other areas of my responsibility, such as physical education and home economics, presented less straightfoiward challenges and rather rare adventures.

It seemed very strange indeed that the position of supervisor of physical education was included in my assignment. I had made no bones about being an athletic moron, I never took part in the conversations about goals or scores when socializing near the water fountain, and I had never attended a hockey game. What was this?

If I thought the appointment was strange, imagine how the physical education teachers looked upon this seeming charade. The day after the announcement was made public, a delegation of the physical education department heads appeared in my office. What a strong, insistent lobby group they were: young, fit and tanned. This appeared to me to be an assault that demanded defence from behind my desk. But in truth, the requests of these teacher leaders were reasonable and the emissaries were quickly convinced that I envisioned my role to be that of an advocate and a support for them in their particular field. We were at peace and we worked well together. By the time the first year was over, they gave me "The Award of the Silver Slipper" — a high high-heeled sandal with thumb tacks pushed through the sole from the inside to simulate cleats, then sprayed silver and mounted on a piece of plywood. It was quite wonderful to be teased in that way. I cried.

The home economics teachers in the secondary schools had one or two champions who thought their subject area should have some attention from the central administration. The point was well taken: their counterparts, the industrial education teachers, were represented at the district level by a consultant, but no one had been assigned to the home economics group — ever. I was asked if I would meet with this particular group and at least recognize these teachers as a viable part of the system.

I remembered my own secondary school days when home economics was considered a Mickey Mouse course. I had learned some things about cooking and sewing that I did not learn at home, but I hardly thought of that course as consisting of much more than hobby crafts. The programs could hardly be considered equivalent to other electives within the school like French, band, art or industrial education. All in all, I did not take on this subject area with a glad heart.

I bungled immediately. I had an old friend who taught sewing and so, as a starting point for my new assignment and to find out the lay of the land, I went to see her. By the time I got back to my office after taking her to lunch, there was a strident voice on the phone. Why was I going to consult with one particular member of their group, not even an active member, and seeking direction from her? Curses. I told the voice why I had visited with my friend, that my only mission was to make a start at finding out how I could help home economics teachers and that maybe she, the voice, could help me to represent her colleagues to their advantage. In time, I learned to respect this forthright person and she did indeed help me to be an advocate for her colleagues.

We agreed that the industrial education teachers had a lot of visibility which home economics teachers did not. In various malls in the city centres, there were often displays of woodwork, beautiful carvings or well-crafted furniture, but who ever saw the beautiful work that the teenage girls produced in their home economics classes? Soon some of the sewing teachers organized a fashion show where work from any participating school would be modeled by the student crafters themselves. In order to increase interest in the show, clothes from one of the most expensive boutiques in the area would also be modeled. Perfect. But then the leaders told me that, because I had been responsible for getting this started, it would only be fair for me to be one of the models. I was speechless. How could I prepare for that?

I called on a drama teacher who I thought would be kind and asked her if she would teach me how to walk. When I had explained my predicament, she advised me, "Go to a local modeling agency and take some lessons." "What a preposterous idea," I thought, "but what fun." And I did just that. With the other aspiring models less than half my age, it was more than a little strange for me to be learning how to twist and turn and present clothes on a catwalk, but I soon learned that people who go in for this kind of training must be, for the most part, centred on how *they* look and not at all bothered with anyone else's appearance. Meanwhile, I gained some confidence and learned how to move. I remembered my childhood role model and how elegant and pretty she looked. In no way did I look like that long-legged, high-heeled blonde beauty but by now I knew that some dreams are never more than fantasies. And anyway, this modeling was only a game.

Modeling clothes may have been a game, but being a role model for women who aspired to administrative positions was not. I was a forerunner as a female school principal in both elementary and secondary schools and with my particular responsibilities on the district staff. I knew that I had received enormous help from people who were in positions to push me on, and I was keen to give the same kind of encouragement to able women that I knew. In my role, I did not have direct power to give anyone a boost onto the administration ladder, but I thought I could help at least a few women to find their own power and to believe in their capacity to extend themselves if they wanted to do that. Someone had told me that there is nothing as helpful as someone who is actually in a leadership role talking about the challenges and opportunities that they have met. I was also told that women have to help one another to reach for the top. With these admonitions in mind, I formed a support group of women that I had come to know in my work. We discussed our ambitions and our goals and we listened to guests whom we invited to give us advice. Not all of the women took a leadership path, but those who didn't were loyal supporters of those who did. I was happy to have found a way to pass on some of the help I had been given.

I have dubbed these "the best career years." Why so? Probably most of all because, during these six years, there were great opportunities to interact with my colleagues: the teachers, the school administrators, the other supervisors and the central office staff. The idea came to us, for instance, that we could set up a professional development seminar in the summer that would be inspirational for educators from across the district and even the province. It would be designed to dissolve hierarchies and geographical boundaries so that the best educational ideas of all sectors would be developed for the benefit of all of us. A great synergy would emerge. Good brains and ready workers from across the district put just such a seminar together and what we called "Summer Ensemble" was born. For two summers in a row, this cross-fertilizing seminar was an outstanding success.

In the spring of 1986, as I started to focus upon the next year's work, I felt as if I had released all of my creative energy in the space where I was. I thought, "I don't want to do this job anymore. It has been fulfilling, has given me a sense of achievement — a very satisfying *Something to Do* — but it has run its course. I am fifty-eight years old; it's a good time to retire from this work."

And so I did.

Retiring

Within a few months of retirement, I had become tired of my purposeless state. It seemed to me that all the things that I did each day I used to do outside of working hours. Now going to the bank was a morning's work. I did some entertaining and joined a gym class. Not enough. Of course, it was the *Something to Do* that was missing: something that would result in a sense of achievement. So I thought about the ambitions I had not fulfilled and about the things I enjoyed doing most, and it wasn't a big jump to decide to continue to study.

Academe was a comfortable milieu for me. I enjoyed the smell of the musty books in the library, the unhealthy food in the cafeteria, the sterile lecture rooms. I loved all of it. So I returned once more to UBC to embark upon four years of course work, seminars, research and writing — all pointing to a doctor of education degree. People I told about this project thought I had gone mad. Didn't I know that further education was undertaken for the sake of getting a better job, or at least better pay? What on earth was I doing, retired and beginning now to work on a doctorate? My response was that this project was the culmination of my work in the field of education and a learning mountain yet unclimbed. In my case, it was the end of a career, not the beginning.

I was, of course, older than any other student — probably older than any other student that had ever enrolled in the program — but I had been an "odd man out" before so that didn't bother me. It did annoy me to be treated as part of a lesser group, of a decidedly lower status

Beth and George, 1991

from the one I had just left. I thought that educators had advanced
to the point where the student should garner as much respect as the
teacher. That did not appear to have happened. It also annoyed me
when I was told that fifty percent of doctoral students in education did
not complete their degrees. Was it really that difficult? Or were the
students not given enough encouragement and help? I did feel somewhat critical of the lack of any feeling of collegiality between graduate
students and the staff of professors. But then, I had been extremely
critical of the professors in my very first year in the faculty of education
at the University of Saskatchewan, hadn't I? Best to just settle down
and get to work.

Twelve years earlier, during my master's program work, I had met
and appreciated the professor whom I called "The Sage on the Stage."
Dr. Graham Kelsey rather enjoyed the alias that I gave him. He liked
to perform and he did it well. Nothing pleased him more than to be
standing behind a lectern or walking up and down a platform, presenting his knowledge of this theory of education or that one. His clipped
Cambridge English was unquestionably correct and his flare for the
dramatic gave weight to his presentations. I was not now, however,
interested in his thespian skills; I wanted to make use of his wisdom,
so I asked him to be my advisor for my doctoral work. He agreed.
Dr. Kelsey was supportive and encouraging and he always made time
to meet with me.

Sage and I worked together happily enough. He was surprised at
how steadily I worked, believing perhaps that I had intended to look on
this project as a hobby for a retired person. But hard as I worked, I did
not finish the degree as quickly as I thought I would. It took four years.
It was encouraging, though, to be awarded (with Dr. Kelsey's help) a
bursary for $13,000 after my second year on the program. I had never
dreamed of receiving that much money as an encouragement to keep
on attending university, the very thing I wanted to do anyway. What a
pot of gold that bursary would have been when I was nineteen!

After the basis of my study — "Teacher Expertise and How It is
Achieved" — had been approved, Sage turned me loose for one whole
summer; he just said to go ahead with the writing and see where it

took me. In September, he tore apart almost all of it. I was devastated. And angry that he had not given me more direction along the way. But he was convinced that this was the way for a student to learn. Maybe he was right.

I pulled myself together and managed to keep rewriting through the following winter. In the spring, Sage judged the dissertation ready for submission. When its defence was accepted and the comprehensive exams completed, Dr. Kelsey was the first to call me Dr. Rowles.

That was a very good year, 1991. Not only was it the year I completed my doctorate but, much more important, it was the year George and I were married.

In 1991, I was sixty-three years old, George Scott was sixty-six. We have discovered that people who are at that age or younger like to hear about how we met, how we got to know one another, how we came to be married. They like to learn that finding someone to love at that age happened to us, so it could happen to them, too. Indeed it could. And if they are as lucky as we are, the last years of their lives will be the best years.

George and I had lived within a few blocks of one another for many years and yet our paths had hardly crossed. Why was that? Because we led quite different lives. My contact with George was minimal and not significant for either of us, although a bit of St. Elmo's fire did flash between us one Friday evening when we were having dinner with mutual friends. The evening was not spectacular except for a stray bit of conversation between us. Neither of us can remember the topic, but both of us can well remember the moment. Our friends at the dinner table didn't notice that the room had lit up. Then George and I went away to our separate lives.

When George's wife died a few years later, I checked him out. I asked an old friend, Vin, about him. Vin said, "Well, just sit and listen to him for a while. George is a great talker and he'll soon be telling you stories that you can piece together until you know all about him. He'll tell you about his attempt to climb the Matterhorn, how he failed and how he had to come home and eat crow after bragging about what he was going to do. He'll tell you about some of his court cases, explaining first that lawyers will only tell you about the cases they have won. He will want you to see the totem poles he carved during his carving phase, and the small figures he fashioned from soapstone. He will talk about hiking and skiing and scuba diving. Just listen to him, Beth," he said. I did listen to him and found that we had much in common, from our prairie roots to our love of the outdoors.

George carried my books when I went to sweat over the defence of my dissertation and he came to my graduation ceremony. My friends thought there was clearly something in the wind.

Several women hovered around George. His eligibility level was high: good looking, a little extra money, a non-drinker and a family man with children long ago fledged and out of the nest. No wonder he was being pursued. As our relationship became closer, I kept telling myself that I must just enjoy the nice times we were having together and not anticipate any serious outcome.

One time, I was set back upon my heels. George invited me to an event and then in another day or so told me that he had inadvertently invited another woman to the same event. I was pretty annoyed and thought to myself, "So much for this guy's attention and priorities." But I presented nonchalance and said to him, "Never mind. I don't sweat the small stuff." Unbeknownst to me at the time, by my apparent composure I had shot up my courtability status by a number of points. When this and other minor glitches threatened, I had to hug my safe little house close around me and spend lots of time with my friends.

George suggested that we could go on a "Wilderness Adventure." I didn't realize at the time that this adventure was a set-up, a test of my acceptance of a roughing-it holiday in contrast to what George believed were my expensive, soft-bed journeys. He had been impressed, for instance, with an Easter excursion I had embarked upon in an earlier life, going to London to see a Constable exhibition, and going to Paris another time on an opera tour.

George thought it would be a great adventure to go to a dude ranch in the mountainous Cariboo country. I must have been bragging about my quarter horse, Belle, which probably gave him the idea. I wished I had kept my mouth shut about Belle, for I did not relish the idea of madcap dashes across great green ranges on what I envisioned would be a skinny, newly retired race horse. Could I possibly handle this? Would this challenge be like the horse in my gym class in secondary school? Should I invent an illness? No, I would go.

The test began in an unexpected way and sooner than I expected. George gave me the most beautiful cowgirl hat in the world — a felt folly that must have cost him a pretty penny. It was classy enough that it could have been effective heralding an entry for someone attending the Calgary Stampede. But for me to wear it in earnest in the back country? I jammed on a wide smile to show pleasure, not the dismay I felt when he unveiled his carefully chosen gift. I was convinced that I would look outlandish in this garb. Well, I was dead wrong. The hat was perfect in every way. It looked so good and worked so well for the whole adventure that I took it off only to go to bed. But I'm ahead of myself.

We drove north and west into the Chilcotin mountain country. My eyes grew round when we reached our interim destination, a picture-perfect lodge made of skinned yellow cedar logs, looking like a gracious ranch house fit for the rich and famous. The inside was designed to look rustic, with a huge stone fireplace, heavy pine furniture and a grand central staircase.

Soon after we arrived the dinner bell rang. We swanned down the great staircase to a large, large table, occupied by only a middle-aged cowboy who would get us outfitted, a skinny thirteen-year-old girl who was to be our wrangler, and our sixty-nine-year-old hostess who was clearly in charge of operations. The cowboy and the wrangler wore their great hats to dinner. I did not wear mine, but for the first time I realized how dashing it was. Dinner comprised an assembly of leftovers from the previous day's dinner — cold fried chicken, potato salad, large rolls — hardly gourmet, but certainly hearty and a precursor of the meals that were to follow.

Breakfast food was predictable, but the pervading atmosphere was not: the general air of relaxation, the lack of the up-and-at-it country bearing, the absence of the frontier spirit was unexpected. We had anticipated an early rush of ranch routine instead of this holiday-like milieu.

Cariboo adventure: Wrangler, Beth and George

After some time, Cowboy found horses for each of us and we managed, with a little help, to get ourselves in the saddles. I felt that I looked outstanding in my beautiful hat, but otherwise I did not feel so great, mostly because I was not at all comfortable on that horse. He was called Warrior and he looked like a war machine — a Sherman tank. Once astride him, with my legs splayed out across his great back, I felt as if I were riding my grand piano. I can't think of a less likely mount for me, but determined to be sporting I rode off into combat like a good soldier.

George's horse was called Love Boat, a name that incited immediate laughter even before we heard George yelp when she stepped on his feet and growl when she snapped at his hand. She was a tad long in the tooth and did not appear to be ecstatic about carrying this dude up the mountain. She was a morning crank. But George was not. Every now and then he would burst into a cowboy dirge learned in his youth, fourteen verses long and all produced with a high-voiced twang:

> Oh, I have no use for the womin',
> A true one will never be found.
> They marry a man for his money
> When it's gone, they'll turn him down.
> My pal was an honest young cowboy,
> Honest and upright and true.
> He turned to a hard-shootin' gunman
> On account of a girl named Lou.

George and I, with Hostess, Cowboy and Wrangler, sat those horses for four hours until we reached our outpost, a cabin on Potato Mountain. This safari bore no relation to the dude-ranch riding I had envisioned. During the four hours, never once did Warrior grind out of his lowest gear, never once did he even think of a trot, let alone a canter. We were heading right through bush country, over rocks and little rills with tree branches swiping at us all along the way. This was not ranch country with rolling grassy hills; this assault was upon a mountain.

Cowboy led us along a hardly discernible trail, up and up, around huge rocks and along the sides of streams. Every now and then — perhaps once each hour — we would stop to give the horses a rest and then we could dismount and take time to see details of the undergrowth, the trees and the small flowers. Then we would climb and wriggle back up onto the beasts. But throughout, the hat was outstanding. Whenever Warrior plowed between trees or when branches came straight at me, I'd just put my chin down so that my lovely hat took the brunt of the attack. It never wavered nor did it show any signs of abuse.

A final lift of my chin and there was our cabin: a mountain cottage with a burned patch of ground in front of it that marked the spot for our campfire. Dismounting with a certain lack of grace and managing to stand upright after several bow-legged attempts, we took stock of what lay before us. Just down a little track was the outdoor toilet, a welcome sight.

Hostess, with George's urging, got a fire going to brew coffee. Cowboy tethered the extra horses he had led in a train behind him and then almost immediately started the return journey to the lodge, much sooner than little Wrangler would have liked. So there we were for the next four days: Hostess, Wrangler, George and Beth.

The cabin, attached to a large veranda, comprised one large room and a loft. George and I were encouraged to climb up the ladder to the loft, set some pieces of foam rubber together and lay out our sleeping bags. The foam rubber pieces were small and in oddly uneven shapes, like the pieces of a jig-saw puzzle. "You can't keep out the rats, you know," said Hostess. Ugh.

The quite-old woman (old for her job, at least) and the quite-young girl set up a tent outside for their sleeping quarters; the cabin was for George and me and the rats. That was fine during daylight hours, for we spent almost no time indoors, but at nightfall we felt that we were going into battle. The ladder wobbled and its steps were unevenly spaced, and every night we had to climb up and down more than once. Why is it that, as soon as conditions are difficult, it is always necessary to get up in the night to void? It happens on boats and it happened in that cabin. What a performance: to find our boots, shake them in case they were housing a rat, pull them on over bare feet, find the top of the ladder, careen down all six rungs, stumble outside and down the little path, and then produce very little indeed to make it worthwhile. Every night.

One of the horses that Cowboy had led up the mountain, Lucky, proved to be a much more suitable mount for me than the intrepid Warrior. Lucky was a bit tall for me to mount, but I was not too proud to accept help and once in the saddle I could sit her comfortably. We were a merry company. We never seemed to make a sortie out of the camp until afternoon, but then each day of riding over Potato Mountain brought a feast of spectacular views, an abundance of wildlife and the glory of high-country air. We rode far above the treeline so that we could see over the mountains and valleys for miles and miles. There were deer, antelope, mountain sheep, ptarmigan and grouse. Each day was an adventure.

On the fourth evening George asked me how I liked this kind of travel. I replied, "It's grand. I'm enjoying it a lot. Next stop, the Four Seasons Hotel." Of course I didn't mean it: I had never enjoyed a holiday more. The wilderness adventure was a prelude to many happy days. But, sad to say, I never again wore my spectacular hat.

Wedding and Honeymoon

On Labour Day, the first of September, George asked me if I would consider going with him to Maui later in the fall, staying there for four or five months and then going to Europe for a few weeks in the spring. I equivocated a little, explaining to him that this would necessitate making some major changes in my life: I would not be able to continue my commitment as the church organist, I would need to arrange for someone to look after my sweet little house, I would have to reject an offer to teach at the University of British Columbia. Maybe a month or two away from home would work for me, but I would have to take time to consider going away with him for a whole winter.

I had not intended that these riders on his idea would precipitate George's response. He asked me to marry him. Well. That was a very different proposition. I was truly surprised. I had thought that it might happen some day, but not yet. It was a proposal that I accepted immediately.

I was elated. I was *very* elated. I was going to burst into a whole new life with this man that I had come to find exciting and interesting, who said he loved me and whom I was sure I loved. I made another of those sudden decisions, but this time the right one.

We set the date: November 16. What a lot there was to do. First, of course, to tell our friends and relations that we were going to be married. George phoned his daughters and his son right away. One daughter said, "Well now. Something happened over the coffee cups because I was talking to you an hour ago and you didn't mention this." Most of our friends were quite, quite delighted for us — not very surprised — and immediately pitched in to help us move to this new part of our lives.

The first great move was to a new house. George said to me, "Your house is too small for us. Do you want to live in my house?" I said, "No." So now that both of our houses were rejected, we set about looking for a home that would please the two of us. Great fun. We were shown half a dozen houses that were within our stated price range. None pleased us — really none at all — so we changed realtors and found such a beautiful spot that neither of us has ever wanted to leave and here we are still. Right here in Surrey, we have a view of the water that is serenity itself, there are main floor rooms that flow together spaciously, rooms that are homey yet can accommodate large groups, and there is room for an English flower garden. Perfect.

Less than perfect was the job of deciding what to do with the accumulation of things in two houses so that what was left would meld together into a suitable, attractive, comfortable home for a barely united couple, each of whom had special treasures and special needs. What to throw out, what to keep? What to do with the doubles — the two dining room suites, the four sets of bedroom furniture, the endless kitchen tools, books, dishes, linens? We sorted into piles — give away, throw away, move; give away, throw away, move. Pictures, endless pictures. Trips to the store for more boxes to fill with more stuff. But once the move was made, we had all I could possibly dream of for the start of the exciting, special life that was yet to come and the joy that we had no idea would lie ahead of us.

The celebration with our friends and relatives, the parties and dinners, culminated in the wedding day itself. It was a stormy, stormy day. A tree fell across our road, breaking the hydro and phone lines so that we were without power or light for several hours. Still, about sixty people crowded in around us in our new home, by that time well-lit again and warm. We were married by a minister, a dear friend that both of us knew well. George chose as one of the readings, part of Ecclesiastes:

*Go thy way, eat thy bread with joy, and drink thy wine with a merry
heart ... live joyfully with the wife whom thou lovest all the days of
thy life ...*

George and I flew to Maui the day after we were married. The advent
period before our wedding had left us breathless. I didn't find much
time to think about Hawaii. All that I knew or needed to know was that
George had owned a condominium in Maui for many years and that he
was in the habit of spending weeks or months there each winter. Now
he and I would be doing that.

George and his family loved going to Maui and they did so whenever they could. They didn't tell me a lot about it, just rolled their eyes
in such a way that I thought I must be going straight to heaven.

We arrived on this Hawaiian island in the late afternoon, drove
directly to the Kihei Beach area, had a quick look around our winter
home and went immediately to a condo where we were to have dinner
with some of George's friends. No doubt they wanted to have a look at
this woman who had stolen their prize, or at least so it seemed to me.
I have never been good at first meetings and this was one of my worst
performances. I felt as if I were Exhibit A and as if I had inadvertently
entered the wrong contest. *Flinty* again?

This was, however, a holiday haven: warm air, spectacular
beaches, a profusion of birds. Our routine was to spend the mornings
on the beach, lunch at quite exciting spots in various parts of the island,
and laze away the afternoons. I'm not good at lazing so I looked for
a project.

I found a wonderful, old sewing machine that I could coax into
action. Usually I am in too big a hurry to do a very good job of my sewing
projects, but here I took lots of time and turned out some quite nice
Christmas gifts for friends and made a few cool garments for myself
that didn't look too homemade. George was proud of what I could do
and boasted to his friends. I offered myself for the repair of everything
from bathing suits to bedsheets. I earned Maui points and enjoyed the
new challenge.

Eating breakfast on the lanai was one of the especially good things. We could look down at the beach people walking out to claim their favourite spot on the sand and we could see the poolside sunners jockeying for positions on the deck chairs. Our condo unit had an exceptional amount of private outdoor space because of a huge deck as big as the square footage of the condo below. It looked a bit desert-like, so we painted country scenes on the parapet that surrounded the deck and even painted a great rug-like circle on the floor. Here was a special private spot for lounging outdoors at any time of the day and an ideal accommodation for star gazing at night.

George taught me to swim. It was a challenge for him to get this athletic moron to move through the water with any kind of grace, but after a few weeks, working at it every day, he did help me to become comfortable in the water — a fine achievement. Eventually he managed to coach and cajole me until I could propel myself through the water along the length of the beach. George taught me three strokes: the side stroke that was my favourite, a back stroke that was good for resting, and a frog-kicking, arm-thrashing frontal attack on our piece of the Pacific Ocean. Learning self-propulsion through the salty water was a major achievement.

Once I was comfortable in the deep water, George introduced me to snorkelling. That did not go as well. This particular objective was never achieved, for I never did become at ease with the apparatus. Getting flippers onto my feet and then getting myself afloat made for an especially ungainly performance; it was necessary to sit in the water but not far enough into the water to float. It would have helped if my bottom had been flat, but that was something I had avoided all of my life. Further to that, harnessing my mouth, nose and eyes in goggles that extended down over my face to my chin seemed designed to choke me to death even before I flopped out to peer through the deep water. I was a rather disappointing snorkelling pupil; nevertheless I did have a bit of an encounter with the very beautiful fish and coral that abound in those waters, and I did experience the wonders of the underwater world. *National Geographic* pictures come alive for me now.

Another great adventure we undertook was climbing down into

the crater in the middle of Mount Haleakala, working our way across the bottom, emerging on the other side and climbing up to the top again. When we started out early, early in the morning at ten thousand feet, it was cold, so cold. By the time we had stumbled down to the floor of the crater, it was hot, really hot. I'm not keen on feats of physical bravado but I wanted to please George, who assured me that I could manage it. I did.

I did not, however, become adept at beach socializing. I did not enjoy being one of the half-naked old people sitting in a circle on the sand. I felt as awkward as I had as a child moving from a country school to a city school. The problem, of course, was the lack of something to do. Little did I know that, within a short time, George and I would find a very different place for our lives, a different place in the sun.

Happiness: Testing the Formula

The fat little girl from Saskatchewan had surely found happiness now. According to the formula, all of the elements were in place: the *Someone to Love*, the *Something to Do* and the *Something to Look Forward To*. Surely now — at the end of a career, at the end of the coveted education, at the beginning of a marriage — surely now would be a great time to test the validity of the formula.

The *Someone to Love* appeared to be two-fold: one, a loving relationship with many people and two, the special love of a partner. There was a great wealth of the first of these — family, school and work friends, neighbours and many others — all providing places to put my love and to find happiness. I became acutely aware of the value of all of these people to love when, after the end of my first marriage, I lived alone for eleven years. I was certainly lonely at times during those years, but I was never without *Someone to Love*.

As for the second component of *Someone to Love*: the special love of a partner. After taking missteps and making unwise decisions, now with great good luck I had found and married the special someone who brought me love for all the days of my life.

I had already learned to be careful with the *Something to Do*. Before I joined the workforce, I had learned that there needed to be a sense of accomplishment and satisfaction to make the *Something to Do* an effective element of happiness. There had been times when, full of grief either for the loss of Wayne or for the collapse of my first marriage, almost any work would have shoved away unhappiness. For the most part, though, when work was physical drudgery or when it did not lead to a sense of achievement, it did not help to bring happiness. Just having something to do, like the work experienced in the crucible of the laundry in Banff, was not good enough. And later, I had jumped over the fence in Saskatoon when my teaching work there became repetitive and stale, and I had moved from the principalship of the junior secondary school when I was not satisfied that I was making a difference to the education of the students there. On the other hand, creating a home, learning to be a satisfactory teacher, principal and supervisor were things to do that brought a sense of accomplishment and well-being. The *Something to Do* needed attention, and sometimes bold steps had to be taken in order to provide this satisfactory piece of happiness.

But not right now. Right now it was time to adjust to a new life, to ease out of the employment world and the last education spasm and, most important of all, to become part of the George-and-Beth team. The *Something to Do* would have to wait.

As for the *Something to Look Forward To*, it appeared now that fortune had smiled on me. I had days and days of contentment and adventure to look forward to. I had found much happiness.

PART THREE

LATE BLOOMING

*The logo of the African Canadian Continuing
Education Society (ACCES) depicts the
African Acacia Tree set upon a leaf of the
Canadian Maple. The African tree is also
called the Whistling Thorn, an apt symbol of
cheerfulness amidst discomfort.*

Hooked

I was in a cocoon: in as safe and secure a place as I had ever known, surrounded by a beautiful home and George's love. What more could anyone want?

Physically, nothing at all; psychologically, though, wider boundaries. I became aware that I needed to move out of this casing which had become too small a space for comfort. Long ago, when the classroom walls seemed to be confining and when the school building became inhibiting, I needed to push out. Once again, I needed more space and more challenge. Once again, I did break out — this time into a whole world of space, a great, exciting new territory. It happened by chance. Or was it really by chance?

In January 1993, George and I came upon a book written by Robert Rodale: *Save Three Lives*. Rodale's book had a profound effect upon both of us.

Rodale talked about poverty and starvation in third world countries and about the importance of addressing these problems early enough and in such a manner that they would not continue to recur time and time again. Rodale's premise was that indigenous people, by using their own knowledge of their own environment, can be helped to sustain themselves so that they can grow enough food for themselves and their families. Rodale believed that if each one of us were to help one family to sustain itself, we could "save three lives."

Was Rodale saying that George and I, for instance, might be able to save lives and what is more, by convincing other people to join us, save *many* lives? Why wouldn't we do this? We had time and energy and I was especially ready for a project that would give me a sense of usefulness and achievement — *Something to Do*. George, although he said many times that he would have been happy just to spend his winters in Hawaii and his summers in the garden at home, stepped forth with gusto and commitment. He will still tell people sometimes, "It's that damn Beth. She just has to be *doing* something. She's the one who got us into this." I take that as a compliment. George is no victim.

As soon as we returned home from Maui in April that year, we wrote letters and visited agencies that were providing foreign aid. Nothing seemed to come of it. We knew that we didn't want to work in a third world country and that we were not knowledgeable about Rodale's field, agriculture. And we did not want to hand out leaflets or answer the phone in the office of some well-established organization. When we did make offers of our services in *our* fields — law and education — there were no takers. Here we had thought we were valuable commodities that would be embraced with gratitude and put to use at least as recyclables. That wasn't happening. Although humbled, we were not deterred. We *would* save three lives.

Then we heard about the Canadian Harambee Education Society (CHES).

CHES was founded by Lorrie Williams in 1985. The story of the beginning of CHES is a credit to the determination of this astounding woman. Lorrie spent a year in Kenya, teaching in a secondary school. One of her assignments was to "chase" students home when their fees were overdue — a heart-rending thing to have to do, especially when the student was learning well and when "chasing" someone home was an apt description of what was being done. The students desperately wanted to stay in school. And Lorrie knew that education was the best and perhaps only means for people to climb out of poverty.

The first time Lorrie was confronted with this chasing requirement, she paid the fees herself; the second time, she asked her mother to send money for rescue. Lorrie made up her mind that when she returned to Canada she would see what she could do to help needy, well-achieving students to stay in secondary school. She established CHES as a registered non-governmental organization, an NGO.

Save Three Lives? CHES was saving many more than three lives.

We thought we would see if CHES needed our help. We phoned Lorrie, who said she didn't have time to see us but we would be welcome to attend her annual meeting the next Saturday. Once again we felt like garage sale items, but we went to the meeting.

What CHES was doing astounded us. This small organization was giving forty new scholarships each year to bright, needy secondary students who would never have gone to school without the help of Lorrie and her loyal supporters. At that very meeting, we became supporters ourselves. What was more, Lorrie decided that we might be serviceable after all and agreed to meet with us.

Lorrie said that the very best thing we could do to help her would be to start another NGO to ensure that students whose secondary schooling had been supported by CHES could go on to post-secondary education. Well, we could do that. We told Lorrie we *would* do that!

We practically flew home in the car, thrilled with our new-found objective. Lorrie was pleased, too. As she told us later, she performed a little dance when we phoned the next day to tell her that we would follow through on her proposition.

Our project was at hand. Little did we know how it would commandeer our days and how we had discovered a *Something to Do* that would bring us more happiness than anything either of us had done before. We had thought that our lives would comprise the learning years, the working years and then the leisure years. Instead, our retirement combined all of these — learning, working and leisure. This was fulfillment, a joyous time, a bonus.

And so, my story is now infused with tales of our African project. These bonus years harboured other small, personal adventures, too, and so recollections of these incidents are interwoven with those of the new venture that expanded our lives.

Away We Go

We could hardly wait to open the "Africa file." Having an in-house lawyer was a boon. What George didn't know, he knew how to find out. First, he discovered that we required a board of at least five people — three more than George and me — in order to form a society. A long-time, newly retired friend, Gwen Murray, agreed to join us and Lorrie helped us by recommending two women who had experience with CHES. Easy.

Now what would our society be called? CHES TWO? We could do better than that. We batted around the word "continuing" because we planned to continue in the education track that CHES had forged. And "Africa" not "Kenya," because we wanted unlimited scope for our project. George's daughter, Janice, put together "African Canadian Continuing Education Society" — ACCES.

Who would be president? As he often does, George spoke first and in a commanding voice: "I absolutely, under no circumstances, will be president. I will be vice president and you, Beth, will be the president."

Well, I was a little taken aback, but I'm glad it evolved that way. I knew that I could speak softly and that George could carry a big stick.

ACCES was incorporated in October 1993, just short of two years after George and I were married. Rodale had inspired us, Lorrie had mothered us, and our project was under way. We had no idea of how the organization would evolve, what a great number of children and youth would be given a chance at a satisfying life because of it, and how our outreach would extend to people in Canada that we had never even met. We launched the society and, as we took the first step, the second one became clear.

The ACCES board didn't dither around about a mission statement. All of us knew what it was we were going to do — help to alleviate poverty through education — and so we didn't waste time deliberating about that. The mission statement and then the logo, designed by a community college art class, formed the superstructure that housed our policies and supported our philosophy.

In the beginning, we were a kitchen table society: very, very small. We allowed ourselves to be critical of other non-governmental organizations, ones much, much larger than our fledgling society. Perhaps we just envied the donations that these NGOs collected so that they could afford the TV ads and the full-page spreads in the newspapers. We were critical of the photos they used: little children covered with flies and starving people in long, long lines, walking in their rags across endless deserts. We talked amongst ourselves of how pictures of starving people, especially children, get the press and the donations, but responses to these appeals, although certainly necessary, do not solve the underlying problems that result in starvation. We wanted ACCES to provide long-term, sustainable help through funding the development of skills and knowledge so that African people would make lasting changes within their own countries.

We had learned that funding the administrative costs of a society can easily consume fifteen to twenty percent of donations and sometimes even more. Righteous as we might be, we *did* need funds for administration. George came up with the idea of letting people stay in the Maui condo when we did not need it for ourselves or for our family. Instead of rent, we would accept donations to ACCES. Guests always did contribute to ACCES and for a number of years the amount they donated covered our administrative expenses.

By the second ACCES board meeting on December 9, 1993, the society had been incorporated and $1,770 had been received by way of donations — all of it from friends and family. George and I had made the first of several loans to ACCES to keep it afloat. Before Christmas we managed to send out eighty cards with ACCES brochures and letters about our new venture, our African project. A banner headline in the first newsletter in May of the next year proclaimed that "ACCES Presently Supports 29 Post-Secondary Students!"

Gaining momentum was slow at first. When responses to our Christmas mailing began to arrive, we were alternately pleased and disappointed: pleased that so many people were genuinely interested in the project and enthusiastic about what we were trying to do; disappointed that some people were *not* keen and that some told us that our request had come too late for them to add ACCES to the charities they could support that year. It was a lesson for us: this fundraising business was an uphill climb that sometimes spurted ahead, but was never finished and never easy.

But ACCES *was* moving along. We had fun meeting at one another's homes, the recordkeeping was easy, and the encouragement that we received from Kenya made our hearts glad.

George and I decided that, in order to make the project come alive for us, we needed to go to Kenya. We needed to be reassured about the country. Many of the African countries were not politically stable, had negligible infrastructure and were in the throws of economic collapse. Was Kenya really a stable country? What was it like in Kakamega and the rest of Western Province, the part of Kenya where CHES and ACCES were located?

And we needed to meet the students. Were they so poor that even with ACCES supplying their fees and full board, they would not be able to find transportation, books and clothing from their own families and friends? How many students would be anxious to continue their education and what institutions would they want to attend?

We went to Kakamega that first winter to find some answers to our questions. We had no idea how often we would make that journey: that we would do so every second year after that first time. As the years went on, we no longer needed to go to Kenya as we were doing this year, to monitor and evaluate the work there: ACCES became well cared for by our Kenyan partners. But we did need booster shots of inspiration from time to time, and we found this in abundance when we became acquainted with the beautiful people of Kenya.

The Heart of the Matter

At the outset of our odyssey to the centre of the action, we were encumbered with a well-meant gift: four hundred denim shirts. *Four hundred.* We took them with us in four large boxes and, unlikely as it seems, all four boxes arrived in Nairobi when we did. The customs officers were not so pleased to see them. "Open these boxes, please ... Are these new shirts?"

"Yes, they are new, and they are being given away to people who need them."

"You will have to pay duty on these shirts."

"What? They are for gifts. They are for people who cannot afford to buy shirts. They are gifts from Canadians to Kenyans."

"What do you think you are doing for the textile industry of the Kenyan people? Our textile industry has already been almost ruined because of gifts of used clothing from foreigners."

"But this is not used clothing. These are brand new shirts."

"You will pay duty on them or you will leave them here. If you take them, you will need to pay one thousand dollars." $1,000.00!

And that was that. We paid. We calculated that the cost of each free shirt came to $2.50 — still a bargain. But we did learn a lesson. We learned that charity has many faces and that ACCES had better be aware of it. As time went on, we learned that we should not, for instance, carry books to Kenya, books that our friends in Canada no longer want but hate to throw out. Kenya's own publication industry needs to be valued.

It was a long way from the west coast of Canada to Nairobi. Just the nine and a half hours to London was enough, knees almost under chin, arms close to body, ankles swelling — an endurance test for the most stalwart, and we were old enough to be called spry. (*Spry?* How dare they!) But once at Heathrow, there was an eight-hour slump before we could be on our way again — not time enough to go into London, so we waited it out. I stumbled from one outlandishly expensive shop to another: pricing handbags at Harrods, scanning every book at W.H. Smith, snickering at the price of the Bali shoes, one pair equal to the fees and accommodation for an ACCES scholarship student. Each time after my "shopping" trip around the airport, when I returned to the second row of seats at Gate Ten, George would still be in the third seat from the end.

I'd try a cheery warble: "Just two more hours."

"Impossible," he'd growl. We'd start another crossword.

"What's a word for disconsolate?"

"Forlorn?"

"No, five letters." Silence.

Finally, we heard a loud blare close by, "B.A. Flight 295 for Nairobi." We stumbled down the ramp and squeezed into our small space. I eagerly downed a double Scotch that I hoped would put me to sleep. Eight and a half more hours. Difficult. And then customs and the damn shirts.

We were to be met at the Nairobi airport by Festus Litiku, a friend of the CHES people. Of course, we had never met him, but it would not be difficult for him to pick us out. How many senior couples, both with white skin and whiter hair, would be on B.A. Flight 295 at eight in the morning? After the shirt debacle at customs, we waited until we were the only passengers left hanging about. No Festus. We did our best with the phones, glad that English is one of the official languages in Kenya. At last we tracked him down — he had quite forgotten about us. He strode toward us, a plump-ish middle-aged man with a great grin across his face, effusive with greetings and dripping with apologies. He took us at once to his great house to meet his wife, Mary, and to give us cooked curried bananas for lunch. The adventure had begun.

Festus and Mary were welcoming, gracious hosts. They provided a great way-station with their large, squarely constructed, abundantly furnished home and meals that were far too hefty for us. In fact, the Litikus were a little miffed we didn't eat more than we did. After a day or two, Festus leased us his Peugeot for the 150 mile drive to Kakamega.

Before leaving Canada, we had been warned to guard our wallets as if they were our honour and to avoid malarial mosquitoes as if they were lions. To be careful. What we should have been told was to *stay off the roads*. In Kenya, we were in more danger on the terrible roads and in the awful vehicles than we would ever have been from thieves or insects.

Wherever George and I travel, we always lease a car. Because of this, we have been lost in some of the major cities of Europe. Still, George says that he would do as well without his right arm as without a vehicle. So, with never a second thought, we set out boldly in Festus's car and drove ourselves to the ACCES post in Kakamega. After we had assaulted that route, George said, "I'm not going to do this anymore. I'm too rich for this." Of course, he didn't mean that he was too rich; he meant that driving in Kenya was terrifying.

We had been joined in Nairobi by Nora Harrison, the ACCES agent in Kenya. Before she worked with ACCES, Nora had been an agent for CHES and so she knew the road from Nairobi to Kakamega. Nora and George took turns with the driving and I was relegated to the back seat — only slightly miffed because the compensation was the licence to gaze about at will.

Just getting out of Nairobi was a challenge. Almost as many vehicles crowded the roads there as whip around the streets in downtown Vancouver, but many, many of the Nairobi cars were so decrepit and emasculated that they would not have been licensed in Canada. They spewed black exhaust, they jumped along like crazed rabbits, they rattled and squeaked. We witnessed an incident where the motor in a car simply fell out onto the street and the people walking along the road, unfazed, just pushed the chassis and the motor out of the way.

We had so much trouble finding a safe-looking place to park the car and reinforce ourselves with a cup of coffee and a bite to eat, that we decided we would rather just "keep on truckin'." Our stomachs growled and our bladders all but burst before at last we came to the much more rural tea-growing area near Kericho where, beside the road, just as Nora remembered, there was a great faded-glory manor that had been relegated to the status of teahouse. The three of us wound our stiff bodies out of the car-can and gazed at the beautiful hillsides covered with tea plants — the lovely fresh bushes that are dressed in their own special green.

A bit disappointing, that teahouse. It was quite desolate. How about an orange soda and a package of stale potato "crisps"? A neglected washroom with a cracked basin and a toilet that didn't flush took care of our other discomforts. Then we folded ourselves back into the agitator and churned along the road again.

Every few miles we would come upon a small throng of people milling around market stalls roughly constructed from tree branches that held up ratty-looking tarps. Statuesque women carried great flat baskets of bananas; other women, bent double, trudged along under huge loads of firewood. Skinny goats busied themselves with whatever bits they could find to eat and a thin boy with a stick herded a small cow along the ditch where the grass was green. Every person looked thin, almost emaciated; nobody was plump like Festus and Mary. It would have been a desolate scene if it were not for the brilliant colours of the women's cotton dresses and matching head wraps. From my back seat station, I thought, "So many people and all of them so poor. And we think we can do something about alleviating their poverty through education?" I was tired and had a feeling of hopelessness.

A road sign told us that we were crossing the equator. The sun still blazed hot even though it was now low in the sky. We drove past a police station, municipal and provincial buildings, a fuel station and the remnants of the Kakamega market. A few more minutes and we were at our destination, the Golf Hotel.

Since leaving home, we had crossed ten time zones and traveled almost halfway around the world. It was a day or two before we recovered our zest for our African project. Right now, we questioned our sanity and wondered about our endurance. Were we too old for this?

The Fortress Golf

The Golf Hotel hardly looked like a fortress — a two-storey building hugged by the town on the south and west sides and edged by the golf course to the north and east. There was no such thing as a wall or a moat and we didn't see any guns. It wasn't that kind of defence structure at all. But Fortress Golf, as George and I took to calling it, cloistered us from the streets that were so overloaded with pedestrians and bicycles. And there were guards.

The guards were maribu storks: great, hulking birds that were stationed close to the road by the hotel garbage dump. They watched us whenever we came into the hotel and whenever we left it. They stood almost as tall as I did, their magnificent shiny black frock coats compensating for their ugly bald heads and long, unfeathered necks. They were secretive, only now and then emitting a great squawk when they demonstrated their capacity to fly, their three-metre wingspan seeming to flatten the air below as they determinedly gained altitude. Although posing as guards, they appeared to have spying privileges. They seemed to be watching us at night from their perch on top of the great tree that grew in the garden just outside our bedroom window.

The storks didn't know that, as they watched me in the middle of the night, I often watched them, too. I sometimes have nasty sinus headaches for several nights after I have been on a long flight. The sinus problem only causes pain when I lie down and this ache that joins other night terrors is quelled when I sit up, which I often do for an hour or so at a time. So the maribu storks and I stared at one another with suspicion during the night.

I suppose they could hear the dogs too. I thought that I was hearing a chorus of wild animals on our first night at the Golf Hotel, but we learned later that this was a dog choir. We heard these semi-tame beasts almost every night. They, too, were guards. I suppose the poor things have their night terrors, too.

The hotel was fairly named for there was indeed a golf course just behind it. Cattle shared the fairways with the golfers who needed, therefore, to be wary of the unique hazards of cow pies and hoof holes.

We almost always retreated to Fortress Golf at sundown. The roads were dangerous after dark, we were told, although we never felt at risk. Wherever we went, George and I stood out like beacons: both of us have white hair and considerably fairer complexions than the residents. But when we walked about in the town, no one paid any attention to us. No one deferred to us, nor did anyone step aside for us.

Certainly the mosquitoes threatened. We were careful to use the mosquito nets that surrounded the beds and to be vigilant about downing our medication to stave off malaria.

The Golf was an especially good retreat for, to my delight, there was no way we could do our own cooking. We had all of our meals in the dining room from where we could watch the other guests — very few tourists, but a number of important-looking Kenyans.

Our eyes popped the first time we saw a bowl, a jug of water, soap and a towel brought to a table for the diners to wash their hands before their meal. I wondered why this seemingly biblical service was not offered to us until I realized that it was a practical ritual, not a religious one; we saw that it was the habit of many Kenyans to eat with their fingers instead of using tools as we do. The bowl and ewer were brought to them to wash their hands before the meal and then again after their meal. I had not seen items like this since I visited Aunt Minnie as a schoolgirl. It seems to me that, whether one eats with one's hands or with tools, this is a lovely hygienic practice that we would do well to emulate.

The food suited us well — except for one piece of steak that George asked to be cooked "medium, not too well done." It's good he didn't try rare. George was so ill later that night that I began to wonder how to arrange to get him taken home and, after the seventh time he struggled back into bed through the mosquito net, how to arrange to have his body taken home. He did eat breakfast the next morning, though.

What did living in this fortress have to do with learning about the heart of ACCES? Very little. At that time, though, we didn't have much choice, because ACCES did not yet have a place of its own and the CHES house was full. On subsequent visits to Kakamega, we stayed in the same building that housed the ACCES office. Then throughout the days, we were directly involved with the people who needed our help and who welcomed us to their country. Staying at the Golf Hotel opened the door to Kenya for us, but it didn't get us far inside. Father Patrick, a friendly priest, did that.

Father Patrick

At the time of our first visit to Kakamega, Father Patrick had served the Catholic community there for twenty-nine years. He probably knew the Luhya people there better than any other non-national that we met — although, in time, we did not accept some of his conclusions about Kenyans.

"When you first come to Kenya, you think everyone here is marvellous. In a few years, you think no one is any good at all. After that, you just don't give a damn." Odd, that, from a priest who had spent his life in Kenya. He revealed more of his conclusions later.

Father Patrick drove around Kakamega in either a ragged old truck or a dusty old car. He looked a bit old and dusty himself. We had met him at the petrol station where we investigated one another, as *musunga* (white people) do in Kakamega, for none of us is likely to be there without a particular purpose, Kakamega not being a tourist destination. Father Patrick had just returned from a home visit to Ireland and he was full of energy and vivacity. He told George and me that we should pay him a visit at his rectory.

George said to him, "That isn't good enough. If you want us to visit you, you'll have to set a date and then it will happen." George has a certain blunt way of approaching people that I sometimes find disconcerting, but Father Patrick didn't miss a beat. We were told to arrive in time for dinner that very Saturday evening, to stay the night, and then to go with him to one of his parish churches on Sunday morning.

Two other Canadians, who were staying at CHES House at the time, took advantage of George's brashness and manoeuvred their way into the party.

We were surprised that the priest had offered to host all of us. Did someone in this sparsely supplied and poorly equipped country have space for four overnight guests and could he provide dinner for all of us? Well, indeed so on both counts.

Our new friend picked us up in his abused car and bounced and jarred us over the fifteen miles of "red road" to his rectory. Because the soil in this part of Western Province is a reddish colour, the side streets and country roads are designated as "red roads." They are deeply grooved from the erosion caused by the heavy rains that empty the skies almost every day in the rainy season. When the roads are dry, the ruts grab the car wheels much the same way the streetcar tracks used to grab our bicycle tires and send us in the wrong direction when we were delivering vegetables from our market garden. When the red roads are awash after the rains, no one dares to drive on them.

The rectory was an impressive-looking house, positioned between a girls' residential school on one side and a large cathedral on the other. Before we went inside the church house, we chatted with some of the girls who were draped around and over the fences, barriers that either kept them in or us out of the school compound. I remember them as a jolly lot, not shy and not unlike our Canadian teenagers, some of them bold and most of them curious. Our host cleared them out of our way, guided us inside his home and showed us to our bedrooms.

George and I were assigned to a room with two simple cot-like beds. The rest of the room was as sparse as a seminary student's room, but it was certainly adequate and the bathroom was nearby. Father Patrick whisked away the other two guests to another part of the house. "Dinner will be served in half an hour," he informed us.

Dinner bowled us over. What a marvellous production in this seemingly isolated spot that we called the third world. The table sported a sparkling white cloth, the napkins were starched and sprucely ironed, and a pretty flower arrangement set off the impeccable place settings. We ate roast of pork with mashed potatoes and gravy, with apple sauce on the side. I don't remember the rest of the main course, but I cannot forget the dessert — apple pie, one of the best I've ever eaten, served with slices of sharp cheddar cheese. The whole feast was presented quietly and efficiently by the cook himself, backed up by a female assistant whom we caught a glimpse of now and then in the kitchen doorway. Not a very tough post for this missionary — very accommodating, in fact. But wasn't there a remnant of colonialism here?

At dinner and later, when he took us into the lounge, our host regaled us with stories about the Luhya people that he served. He was a marvellous raconteur, drifting without prompting from one story to another. We were in his thrall for hours.

In the morning, after making our ablutions we drifted around, waiting for something to happen. After a little time, the cook welcomed us into the dining room and offered us fruit, bacon and eggs, toast and coffee. But where was Father Patrick? Eventually he burst in upon us, apologizing for his lapse of courtesy. He said, "I had to marry a couple of people out there." We gawked. The priest explained that it was very important for this rite to be sanctified in short order for the protection of the woman's right to ownership of her part of the land where she and the man were living. Again, we were entranced.

All of us went with Father Patrick for morning mass at one of his parish churches. The church was a mud-daub building, low on the ground with a dirt floor and tiny openings for windows. We would encounter many similar buildings in the years to come.

Entering from the blazing sunlight, we couldn't see a thing. After a minute or two, we could discern rows of simple benches and a rough-cut lectern in front of them. Sixty or seventy people were sitting on the benches, some of them hurrying to set seats for us in a separate place near the front of the building. We didn't like sitting apart in honorary seats, but we couldn't pretend that we weren't different — four very white faces amongst all of those black ones. Anyway, where we were seated was a good viewpoint from which to see both the leader and the people.

Father Patrick had warned us that we would not understand a word of the service because it would all be in the Luhya language.

True, we did not know the words, but there was much that we did understand. Most of the people were very poorly dressed: a man whose jacket had one sleeve half ripped off at the shoulder, another with ragged pants that would fit his big brother. Some women did wear beautiful, colourful matching hat and dress outfits, but they were few and far between. What was unforgettable was the devotion that emanated from them, both in their demeanour and in their fervent singing. It was one of the first times I had heard women ululate and it sent shivers up and down my spine.

The priest encouraged members of the congregation to participate in his homily and from time to time they did. He listened to them respectfully and appeared to enlarge upon what they said. He made a conversation of his message.

I thought how very wonderful was their faith. They had so little to look forward to in this life; at least they could look forward to their Heaven and their Jesus. The words spoken or sung in the service did not reach us; the setting and the body language spoke eloquently. At the end of the mass, every single person in the congregation shook hands with each one of us.

We were still a bit overwhelmed with it all when Father Patrick deposited us at our hotel. We had come to Kenya to learn about the people who needed our help. Here was an unforgettable picture of the great poverty we hoped to alleviate.

And we had witnessed more than that. We had seen vestiges of colonialism in Kenya. Father Patrick had exposed us to two of its faces: the very needy condition of the native people and the very comfortable state of the white people. Later on, George and I became aware that ACCES was also colonialist in its management. It was several years before we set that right.

One Student at a Time

What were we doing here? This was not supposed to be a tourist junket, but an excursion to investigate Project ACCES: to find out the effectiveness of the society to which we had committed our senior years; to see where the dollars we had gathered were going and how effectively they were being used. Fortress Golf provided comfortable enough accommodation (though not like the five star hotels that George had once accused me of frequenting) and the visit with Father Patrick was an adventure, but what we had seen and done had not been empowering for our work with ACCES. Where were the students who were receiving ACCES scholarships and what difference was ACCES making in their lives? That's what we wanted to investigate. It did happen, and only a few days after we arrived.

One morning when we were at breakfast, a waiter came to our table to tell us that there was someone in the lobby who wanted to see us. We gobbled our eggs and went to investigate.

It was James Otieno, a young man about five-foot-six, very slight, quiet and intense. He was enrolled in an accounting program at Nairobi University on the strength of a $400 ACCES scholarship. James wanted something more: books and manuals so that he could complete his chartered accountant's certificate at the same time as studying for his accounting degree. It would cost just fifty dollars to help him make double time while he was at university. We got James the funds, of course. He kept in touch with us so that we learned later that he had graduated with distinction and had become a government auditor. On one of our return visits, James invited us to his *shamba* to see his mud-daub house and to meet his wife, who did not speak English. (This was a surprise to us, as they lived close to Kakamega where our English was always understood.) The couple had a two-year-old child who screamed when he saw us: our white faces scared him.

We saw many more students that year and followed the lives of many of them in the next years when we came to Kakamega. One student at a time, George and I and the members of ACCES were confirming Rodale's premise that any of us, even retired people like George and me, could *save three lives*, not directly by warding off immediate starvation, but continuously by giving people the means to provide for themselves. And the rescue would extend further than that. We had learned from our friendly priest and others that Kenyans have very strong bonds within their families: when one family member finds a way to make a living, that person is required to help other members of the family. A scholarship reached far beyond a single student. This was new knowledge for us and further confirmation that ACCES would be productive.

I had spent all of my working years in the education field. Now, with my husband as lieutenant, I was offering to brilliant young people a chance at the education that they could not have achieved without help. We were repeatedly amazed at their fortitude and perseverance. Let me tell you the tale of Godfrey Musila.

Godfrey told us that he realized that "if you live in Kenya, education is the way to climb the ladder of success out of the pit of poverty that most Kenyans find themselves in."

When we met Godfrey he was studying law at Nairobi University with the help of an ACCES scholarship. He's a slim young man. Soft-spoken. He did not appear to me to have the characteristics of a lawyer, at least not the one that I knew best. Events have proven otherwise.

During his third year of law studies, Godfrey joined the Moot Court Club. A moot court is a competition carried out by law schools to test the abilities of law students to carry out their future profession. Godfrey told us that despite his quiet and introverted demeanour, he came across in the moot court situation as very combative and passionate. He was chosen to represent Nairobi University, first in an East African competition on international humanitarian law and then in the All-African competition in Cameroon with one hundred students representing fifty universities. Godfrey was voted the best oralist of the competition.

Godfrey's achievement in the moot court competitions earned him a scholarship to complete his master's of law degree in human rights at the University of Pretoria in South Africa. Soon after, he wrote to us in Canada:

> I have some good news I received five days ago. I am very elated. I have secured a fully funded 6 months internship with the UN International Tribunal for Rwanda (UNICTR) in Arusha, Tanzania, starting January 2005. The internship is funded by the UN. This is particularly important for me because it seems that I am starting out on a path I have so much wanted to follow — international criminal law. I intend to pursue a doctorate in this area. I know that if I work at it, I can be the best international lawyer that I can be. I figure that I am one lucky dude because almost everyone in my class applied, plus many other people and it appears that I was the only successful one from my master's in law class.

Godfrey said that he had seen police brutality and people languishing in jail because they didn't know their rights. He realized that they needed legal help. He has also said that Kenya needs a radical, young leadership that will take the responsibility of securing the future of generations to come. What a privilege it is to have been able to help Godfrey on his climb out of poverty! How astounding to have set this process in motion from our comfortable retreat in Canada.

Then there is Justin Mutabera, who was studying for a bachelor of education degree when we first had contact with him. While at university, Justin formed a student society to proselytize about HIV/AIDS. When he graduated, he found a teaching job and organized a community volunteer society for the same purpose. He sought and received support from ACCES for this initiative.

One time, George and I found ourselves in a strange predicament because of Justin's efforts at community education. Timed for when he knew we would be in Kakamega, Justin organized a country fair, replete with a stridently amplified sound system that blasted out information about the causes and prevention of HIV/AIDS. In order to attract many people to the fair, Justin included a soccer match — a sport that is exceedingly attractive to the people of Western Province.

George and I and other dignitaries were seated on special chairs placed under a huge tarp beside the soccer field. We watched as a great crowd, perhaps a thousand people, gathered all around the fence that bounded the field — women with babies slung on their backs, men with toddlers on their shoulders, and teenagers draped on any spot they could find. We agreed that one of us would probably be asked to make a speech. We did not get off so easily.

After a long wait, the athletes of both teams were lined up, great shoulder to great shoulder, facing the front of the guest pavilion where we sat. Then George and I were directed to walk along the lines of players, shaking every player's hand. I felt very small.

I felt even smaller when a voice on the loud loudspeaker declared, "Madam Beth will kick off the ball."

What? Kick off the ball? Me! Kick off the ball! Didn't they know that I was athletically challenged?

Beside me in the guest line-up stood a lovely Kenyan gentle-man who coached me as the speakers blasted out two or three more announcements.

"You'll have to make a little speech, you know," said my coach. "Just welcome the teams and wish them a good game. Then you'll kick the ball."

"I can't kick the ball. I can't. I'll fall on my head."

"Sure you can. You don't have to kick it far at all. I won't let you fall on your head."

"Can I hold the ball while I kick it?"

"No, no. You must drop it. You can do that."

Coach didn't know the worst of it: that one of my feet had been badly injured in a car accident many years ago. It was fine for walking, but for kicking a huge ball? Or for standing on, while I kicked the huge ball with the good foot? I'm sure I don't know which I did, but somehow the ball traveled a few feet from us and that seemed to be all that was expected anyway. Coach patted my shoulder. Justin seemed to be satisfied.

The soccer game event makes us laugh whenever we think of it. More important, though, is the way our hearts swell when we remember meeting and following the lives of many of the thousand or so young Kenyans who have benefited from ACCES scholarships — like James and Godfrey and Justin.

George and I received a special treat one day from Justin. He asked us to speak a few words of encouragement to his volunteers. But after we had done that, we were the ones who received the encouragement. Justin gave each of us a name in Kiswahili: George was called *Olwanda* which means "rock" and I was to be *Nuru*, the word for "light." I thought George's name suited him very well — he was certainly a rock to me — and I felt loved and flattered to be called a light.

We became aware of one particular light when we visited Kakamega: the light of joy in our lives as we met one student at a time.

A Driving Feat

That first year, in the ex-pat community that we joined in Kakamega, George and the rented car were very popular. Within a couple of days of our arrival, he had taken a young woman with malaria to a medical centre, had driven a CHES agent's guest to the home of her student, and had escorted several ladies to the Kakamega forest. But his greatest driving feat was to take the two of us to the Masai Mara game park.

What a mistake. It is a wonder we did not kill ourselves on the road or get stranded overnight in the car and eaten by a lion. From the very beginning, we were much too naïve and careless. We were not able to find a road map to the park on the Mara River and certainly not to Little Governor's Camp, the safari resort where we had a reservation. The directions we were given, however, seemed fairly straightforward and so away we went.

Ignorance is bliss, is it? Not for us on this perilous journey.

We still thought in terms of highways or at least of main roads, unaware of the vast uncharted veldt that lay ahead. Soon the road just petered out until it became only a track across a vast, flat plane with grey soil and a few wisps of grass. Navigation was questionable. I had been designated navigator.

"Which way, Beth, left or right? Now! Tell me *now*!"

"Left. *Turn left!*" Did I know? I would have a fifty percent chance of success by saying left.

In time we overtook two skinny people, stopped beside them and asked for directions to the Masai Mara. They pointed straight ahead, but of course the road did not go straight ahead. George drove steadfastly on until we blundered into more walkers, three of them this time.

I hissed across to George, "We'll be okay now. Guides aboard." After about a mile, our passengers signalled to us that they would get out now. When we asked for directions they too pointed vaguely ahead. I didn't think they knew where we were headed ultimately, but did they know that just ahead lay — an embankment?! We stumbled right onto a precipice. And over it.

We descended what could only be a streambed. Just rocks — large ones, small ones, jagged ones, smooth ones. There didn't seem to be any soil or any roadway at all. The car jolted and leapt from one rock to another, sometimes scraping bottom, sometimes almost getting hung up. We were trapped. We could only go forward, perilously clattering down this embankment, with no end in sight. Then, "I see elephants! Look George, there are elephants down there!"

"Look? How am I supposed to *look*?! I'm trying to keep this damned car from smashing apart!" Bit of stress there.

Of course there was an end eventually. One last horrible lurch and we were back on level ground. Miraculous. The devil's driving test ended on the desert-like bottom land that looked similar to the countryside before we catapulted down the embankment. The daylight was beginning to fade and we were getting truly quite frightened: this was lion country; we had no water or blanket to get through a cold night. But before darkness fell, we managed to reach Little Governor's Camp — well, almost. We were still on the wrong side of the Mara River. Greeters walked across a footbridge to welcome us and to tell us to just drive along the track and in about an hour we would get to the other side of the river where we were to park our car.

George morphed into an ugly tourist. "You just take this car and get it there. Here are the keys." It cost us money, but the next morning the car was safely with us again.

Our journey to the Masai Mara signalled the beginning of the end of our car rental in Kenya, although not the end of our visits to this game park Garden of Eden where giraffes, wildebeest, impala, elephants, so many animals grazed.

Kenya's biggest industry is tourism. Despite what we had been told about respecting their textile industry, it contributes very little to the gross national product when compared with tourism. When anyone travels to Kenya to encounter the ACCES post, we insist that they go to at least one of the game parks. The animals there are part of the Kenya that we love.

At the Masai Mara, we encountered a very different culture from that of the Luhya people who live around Kakamega. People of the Masai tribe live beside the Mara River, just outside the park. They are cattle herders. We saw the tall, slim men, moving huge numbers of cattle close to the river. As tourists, we were encouraged to visit a Masai village and to buy some of the trinkets that the women had made. Their children were certainly covered with flies, but they did not look thin or ill.

Unlike the Luhya people who have a deep desire for education, the Masai do not show any interest in education as we know it. We would not dream of imposing it upon them. We could see how easily Westerners could be seduced into forcing their culture upon indigenous people who appear to be deficient in what we consider to be the necessities of a satisfying life. But we have been mentored by Robert Rodale and we will mind his admonition that it is the native people themselves who must decide what help they need. ACCES will only help people to help themselves.

And what of our perilous journey back to Kakamega? It was not perilous. We were guided by a young man who lives in Kakamega. He directed us to a route that skirted the embankment so that we trundled calmly back to our fortress.

Time to Go Home

Kenya and its people captured our hearts. We had gone to Kenya to gain inspiration for our work in Canada and we found a basket full of it. So we forged ahead. We feared that we were so persistent with our talk of ACCES that our friends and neighbours would duck into doorways when they saw us coming. Gradually our reach extended further. I remember well the first time we received funding from someone we didn't know and didn't know anything about; our own confined circle now overlapped another circle. That was a moment for dancing.

George and I put together a dog-and-pony show that we took on the road. Any collection of people who stood still for a minute became sitting ducks for a broadside of ACCES rhetoric. Our largest assembly comprised a hundred people and our smallest consisted of the one lone university student who had tried to organize the event. That student had heard us speak to a church group and had been so impressed with our passion for ACCES that she thought she could entice at least half of the campus to listen to our pitch. She was our total audience.

For the most part, we were quite pleased with our presentations. Our speeches were carefully scripted, the two of us taking turns, George in his strong assertive voice with hands and arms flailing, me smiling deferentially, my neck stretched out to reach the microphone. It was important to prepare carefully for our target audience. One time we misfired. We talked to a Knights of Columbus group about the need to limit the size of families in Kenya in order to relieve some of the poverty. One or two members of the society took exception to what they thought of as advocacy for birth control. Stony faces reprimanded us. We should have been more thoughtful.

The post mortems sometimes resonated with discouragement. At times I felt as if people thought we were trying to spread a disease. A large man said that he'd like someone to give a scholarship to *his* daughter. More often, though, we dripped with self-satisfaction: George would tell me that he saw tears when I told my story about a waif called Mercy. "You nearly lost it yourself, didn't you?" he said.

One small step at a time, we were making progress, coaxing most of the funding from a growing, stalwart band of contributors. One of the stalwarts said, "The Canadian government uses some of our tax money for international development. Why don't you guys try for some?" So we did. I spent hours — days — putting together a proposal to the Canadian International Development Agency (CIDA) for funding for our program. When I submitted it, we were informed that CIDA does not support scholarships. Thump.

Stalwart told us to try harder. "Get yourselves out there. Schmooze."

"Manipulate, you mean. Do we want to do that?"

"Schmooze, manipulate, whatever. I'm talking about being convincing in a clever way. Call it what you will if it makes you happier."

Stalwart was convincing. We arranged to meet a CIDA manager, took her out for a gourmet lunch and then transported her to her next appointment. It cost us half as much as a one-year scholarship for a student, as well as half a day's work.

"You will not be able to convince CIDA to support scholarships," decreed the schmoozee.

We didn't give up. George and I went to the top. We sought out Dr. Perinbam, the creator of CIDA's Non-Governmental Organization program, the first of its kind in the world. He greeted us warmly, then showed sincere sympathy for our dilemma.

"I set up this department of CIDA myself for the purpose of encouraging groups exactly like yours. What you are doing is *human resource development*. Those are the words you must use today," he said. Lewis Perinbam, we discovered, did not walk in line. With his encouragement, we got busy, rewrote the proposal, had it accepted, and were granted $60,000 a year for three years.

Sixty thousand dollars for three years! Manipulating? Schmoozing? Lesson learned.

We had, in fact, made a lovely friend in Lewis Perinbam. He was a quiet but self-assured, gentle man who led and inspired many people and organizations. He became my international development role model.

Dr. Perinbam did not forget about ACCES. The next time we met him, he was in our home at the Annual General Meeting of ACCES to present me with an award in his name. It was a lovely event for ACCES and especially for me. I was delighted and quite humbled to have the words "imaginative," "leadership" and "international development" applied to me. I'm sure that many of us like to think of ourselves as showing leadership; imaginative leadership was even better. What pleased me more, though, was the designation of "international developer." Once again, we were reminded of Robert Rodale's book, *Save Three Lives*, and his advice to help people to help themselves.

It seemed to us that ACCES had grown beyond the boundaries of a kitchen organization. Our reach now extended to Ottawa, the seat of the Canadian government, and beyond that to the status of an international development organization.

Boating

There is much more to tell about the evolution of ACCES in Kenya and in Canada, but despite our obsession with ACCES, there were times when we left that avocation behind, and engaged in episodes of fun and adventure like those with which our lives together began. Each summer, for instance, there was at least one boating adventure.

Large bodies of water are not familiar or comfortable places for prairie girls, so to go on a sailing odyssey had never been part of my dreams. I did know that the waters of the Gulf Islands in British Columbia provide a playground for thousands of boaters. These waters are not in the open sea for they are well-protected on one side by the west coast of Canada's mainland and on the other side by the quite large land mass of Vancouver Island. Protected as these waters are, though, the waves can become choppy; sometimes storms erupt and the seas become fiendishly angry. In truth, the deep sea and the vast expanse of water seldom become very frightening. It is not the sea that is troublesome: it is the sailboats, with their foolish eccentricities and their unforeseen demands, that make life on board seem borderline hazardous.

The sails, for one thing, need constant attention. When I was told to be helmsman, a significant promotion from the position of deck-hand, and I turned my back on the sails or somehow lost my focus for a mere second, the beautiful billowing sails became limp pieces of cloth, flapping in the breeze. Not good. The captain yelled at me, grabbed the tiller and dispatched me to the galley to make lunch. I wasn't asked

Sailing in British Columbia waters

to take the helm again unless no one else was available: usually when the blessed sails were being struck as we were coming into harbour, or when the wind had become a gale and the whole boat was swaying and creaking so that the other sailors were doing important things to save our lives. In either case, the atmosphere was tense. As helmsman, I was told to keep pointing into the wind. "Into the wind!" hollered the captain. "Can't you feel the wind on your face? Watch the telltales!" The wind was all around us. We were pointing in the wrong direction from where we wanted to go, I knew that much, but I was not encouraged to try to make sense of the orders. This was unpleasant.

I must say in my own defence that as helmsman, I never lost a mast nor caused anyone to fall overboard. But I felt myself to be a slow learner. Shades of failing to leap the horse in the gym.

Sailboats are supposed to be powered by sail and wind. The motor on a sailboat resents the work of propelling the vessel through the water, and easily becomes cranky and dysfunctional. It will not, for instance, abide an errant rope that has fallen overboard and become wound around the propeller. It doesn't realize that extricating such a rope requires major surgery, performed underwater and usually without the help of scuba diving equipment. Neither will the motor contend with the touch of a sandy shore on the boat's bottom side: going aground sends the captain into a spin in which he sends all hands running about in every direction. One boat's motor would not accede to our demand for more revolutions per minute than it had agreed upon. Rather than go faster, it just freaked out with a great blast and we suffered the ignominy of being towed to the next harbour.

Living aboard a sailboat has its challenges, too. It isn't very comfortable. There's a minute amount of space where you can stow your personal bits; the lockers that you do come upon are full to the brim with rain gear, life jackets, ropes, ropes, ropes. The in-the-wayness of almost everything and everybody is perpetually annoying. From bow to stern pieces of boat reach out to clap you on the head or tangle your feet. Only a few precious spots are out of the wind at any time, and they are occupied on a first-to-claim basis. The business of the head — that's the toilet — is unpleasant. Every fart, honk or tinkle you volunteer is amplified as if you were performing on a magnificent stereo set and the audience, your fellow crew members, cannot be more than two or three feet away. The dignity of privacy is denied.

When the weather is foul, dampness creeps into bedding and clothing and nothing really dries out until the sun appears again.

So why do it at all? The sails and the motor are demanding and the available space would make an ant claustrophobic. Doesn't sound very inviting, does it? Well, it *is* inviting. For one thing, seeing the world from the water is quite different from seeing it from the land: as looking down at an object presents another countenance from looking up, so it is with the land and the sea. Perhaps it is like a description in a different language: the perspective has changed.

A better reason to go down to the sea is to interact with people in a different culture. Boaters are unique. Even those of us who are boaters for only a week or two at a time experience quite altered relationships. For the most part boaters are relaxed, less time-conscious, often less energetic than land lubbers. When they are at sea, people are especially ready to help one another, to accept the foolhardy as well as the careful, the bold as well as the timid. There's empathy to spare, as if all of us know that anyone's predicament today could be ours tomorrow and that we are all in the drink together. And for sure there is drink together.

On two occasions, George and I chartered a sailboat in Greece. Now those were outstanding adventures. Each time, we flew to a harbour where a huge flotilla of boats was moored. We were shown to our particular vessel and subjected to an orientation session to which we paid close attention, inspecting the boat meticulously. Even though sailboats are basically alike in their design, there are significant differences between them, differences that can become vitally important to know, especially for those moments of terror. It is essential to understand, for instance, how to switch to another battery when the first one dies, how to read the fuel gauge, how to flush the head.

Each time we sailed into a Greek harbour there was a new challenge. For instance, we were required to nose into a pier, drop the stern anchor just in time to let the bow reach the pier and coordinate this whole operation with the reversal of the motor. During our introduction to the boat our instructor had said, "Once you drop the anchor, you don't have to watch it sink to the bottom." Very funny. Obviously one didn't have to watch it, but knowing about the force of gravity doesn't seem quite enough assurance!

All told, we never rammed another vessel, never propelled ourselves forward so fast that we climbed over the dock, and never swore at one another. But it was close.

Sailing into a small harbour on a Greek island was delightful. Typically there would be a taverna, a small store and a few houses. At the taverna we were sometimes invited into the kitchen to see the particular dish that was being prepared for the evening meal. We'd sit at an oilcloth-covered table and look out to where our boat was moored.

At one of the tavernas, the host was concerned that our craft was not tied up carefully enough in light of his information that a great storm would be upon us that night. He used enough line to truss us up like a Christmas turkey and tied us so securely to the pier that if we had blown away, the dock would have come with us. As it happened, the storm did not materialize.

On one dark night, perfect strangers helped us out of a tight spot when we were in a small harbour, tied to a wharf that was being shared by too many sailboats. It was almost midnight when our aft anchor came free and we began swaying about, banging into boats on either side of us. In almost no time a Danish sailor came to our rescue, rowing our anchor out to plant it in a spot where there was a firm bottom. Meanwhile, a Greek philanthropist tightened our lines against his large vessel so that it held us in a great strong embrace all night long.

George would roar out across the waves the old hymn, "Will your anchor hold in the storms of life, when the billows roll ..." *The anchor did not always hold*. But when the sun shone and we found a strong breeze to fill the sails, we would hurtle along through the warm, shining water. More than once we were at full speed, laughing aloud with pleasure.

In Ireland, we had a quite different boating experience. We had just spent three weeks in Spain, where we had made our way by car across the north of the country from Barcelona to Santiago and back. That odyssey had jaded us with driving a car and staying in a different hotel each night. Still, after flying in to Dublin, we set out valiantly to explore Ireland by car. When we arrived in Athlone on the first day, we found that we could lease a boat for a week and take ourselves down the Shannon River. What a great discovery. We could be on our own, sleep in the same bed more than once and make some simple meals for ourselves. It was another adventure.

This time it wasn't a sailboat that we chartered but a flat-bottomed, motorized riverboat. The two of us had been assigned a bigger boat than we had requested — a tub that had been designed for six. We felt as if we were propelling a barge. Within a couple of hours of starting our journey, we had to get this freighter of ours into a lock. We couldn't avoid it if we were to continue our jaunt down the Shannon River, but here again, as with other boating ventures, there was no end of help. Of course the help was not entirely philanthropic: part of the reason other boaters helped us was self-preservation. Those in the same lock did not want us ricocheting between their boats or bouncing off the cement sides of the lock into their vessels. But we stayed afloat and, by the time we came back upriver to that first lock, we were two of those boaters who were running fore to aft with boathooks on the ready to stave off collisions from the uninitiated.

The Shannon River is beautiful. The banks hardly rise above the surface of the reedy-edged water that is decorated again and again with picture-perfect ballet swans. Often we saw fishermen sitting on camp chairs under the small trees lining the river. In some places, ancient fortresses, incongruous in this peaceful setting, are ensconced on the riverbanks. We could always find a place to tie up and go ashore, once to watch sheep shearing but usually to find food in a pub. Quite idyllic.

Boating adventures have been a delightful part of our lives. Ever since ACCES began, we have had to guard against becoming exclusively absorbed by the business of the society, against becoming "one-note Johnnies." Propelling a boat through various waters requires the focus and energy that takes us away — physically, mentally and even spiritually — from the avocation that sometimes threatens to swallow us. It provides something *else* to do.

On Dry Land Again

When we travel to Kakamega, the closest place we can fly to is Kisumu, Kenya's third-largest city. From Kisumu to Kakamega we must get onto the road — a road that has been the scene of a number of encounters of the worst kind. The distance is only thirty miles, but it can be safely breasted only when the vehicle is armed with at least an hour's time and some ingenuity.

ACCES visitors to Kakamega are asked to arrive in Kisumu on the morning flight so that their journey can be completed in daylight. The taxis that come from Kakamega to meet visitors are in poor shape, their motors unreliable and their chassis abused. These vehicles often break down and when they are *hors de combat* on this road at night, even changing a tire is dangerous. Villains abound. Although many people have cell phones, finding reinforcements is not easy because even your best friend will not want to come out to rescue you after dark.

One visitor to the ACCES project in Kakamega was not able to arrive in Kisumu on the morning flight and because she arrived at night, had a terrifying introduction to Western Province. During her dark ride to Kakamega, a wheel spun off the vehicle, dumped the car askew and vaulted away off into the ditch. It appears that no one was carrying a flashlight or light of any kind. Although there was a spare tire, it had no nuts to bolt it onto the car. The runaway tire was nowhere in sight; though the driver tried to find it, it had just disappeared into the grassy ditch. In time, succumbing to his passenger's pitiful pleas, the driver agreed to abandon the search. He robbed a nut from each of the other three tires, patched on the spare and on they hobbled, each tire now missing one nut.

George and I have never arrived in the evening, but we have nonetheless had harrowing experiences on this road. The worst for us was the time we attacked the road stern first — stern of the car, that is. Kisumu is located by Lake Victoria which is at about sea level; Kakamega, on the other hand, is at 5,000 feet. Much of the altitude to be gained between Kisumu and Kakamega is breached in the first five miles out of Kisumu by way of a long, steep hill that winds up out of Kisumu's flat land. The road is narrow and infested with slow-moving trucks that limp and pant along, constituting hazards for all other vehicles. On one of our journeys up the hill, our taxi balked. The driver tried and tried, but the worn beast just stalled and stalled. The low gears were not in service. Nothing wrong with reverse, however, so before we caught on to what the driver had in mind, he had turned the car around, put it into reverse, and we careened up the hill backwards. Like an elephant running amok, we swerved and leapt and sped past those snails of trucks as we assaulted the hill stern first. George is still annoyed at himself that he did not insist our ride come to an end when we first stalled, halfway up the hill. It was an extremely dangerous manoeuvre. And the tale does not end there.

Once at the top of that first great hill, the taxi was turned to face forward again, but there were still other smaller rises to conquer. We were pushed up one incline by a truck that then puffed past us, leaving us to our own devices. We whooshed down that hill in order to get a running start at the next one.

George was livid. I got the giggles. The relationship became strained.

But there was more. A van tried to tow us with three flimsy strips of rope — which tore with the starting jolt of getting us moving. More rope. More jerks. More breaks. Eventually another passing saviour pushed us and our baggage into his car and drove us to our destination. All he would accept for the favour was a blessing that he did not realize we were not qualified to give. (He was not the first person to think we were missionaries.) When we reached Kakamega all I wanted was two ounces of Scotch. George stomped about, reviewing his decision not to rent a car.

That evening I thought about the business of travel. I remembered how Father had taken vegetables and cattle to Moose Jaw in a wagon, drawn by great farmhorses; how we had a car but could not afford to put it on the road; how I was left to the mercies of a male chauvinist because our muddy roads had deposited our car in a ditch. What was the difference between that Canadian travel and our journey today? Fifty years and another continent. The ingenuity of the Kenyans, patching together their vehicles one way or another, is analogous to the way Saskatchewan farmers pieced their machinery together when I was very young. Eventually the Kenyans too would emerge from their poverty.

Colonialism

After a long history of colonial rule by England, Kenya gained independence in December 1964. For the youthful Kenyans that George and I met, to call someone a "colonialist" was the most derogatory descriptor they could use.

When ACCES began, it was probably necessary to have Canadians manage the ACCES program, setting up systems and arranging procedures so that the funds from Canadian donors could be accounted for to everyone's satisfaction. For this purpose, ACCES selected agents to take care of its work in Kenya. The practice, however, continued for far too long. When we did realize that ACCES, through its Canadian agents, was imposing a Canadian form of colonialism upon its Kenyan organization, we put an end to that system, though not without causing a great ferment amongst some of our supporters.

In the meantime, the returning agents, almost without exception, spoke glowingly of their experience. "Nothing I have done in my life can exceed the experience of working in Kenya," said one. Her partner said, "To see the smiles, the determination and the appreciation of the students made us realize just how important organizations such as CHES and ACCES are in the lives of these young Kenyans."

Accommodation for the agents and space for an office were not easy to find. At first, we had to manage with a small cottage that had no running water, no indoor toilet, no electricity and no telephone. Pretty rough, but there were no complaints at all from the young couple that lived there as agents for one six-month stint. Before the year was out, we were able to rent a very comfortable three-bedroom house at the Kefinco Estate, a Finnish-owned compound nearby.

George and I were delighted to have a bedroom in the Kefinco house whenever we went to Kakamega. Each day we were right in the midst of the ACCES action where one large room served as dining room, living room and office. Food and files mingled together so that certain documents had stains on them from the morning porridge. From my place at the table, my elbow rocked the computer keyboard when I used my knife and fork. The student traffic in and out of that room was fascinating. For us, scholarships were now attached to people who seemed more real than before, their hope and determination already diminishing the grind of their poverty.

The Kefinco house served us very well for three years, but then the estate was sold, the house ACCES rented was put on the market and we were threatened with eviction. Consternation. There wasn't a suitable place to rent in Kakamega.

Festus, our first acquaintance in Kenya, offered to create a place for ACCES, but he could only do so by using our own money. We wanted none of that: ACCES could not afford it, and ACCES did not want to own even a vehicle, let alone a house, in a far-away, foreign country.

"I have enough trouble managing a condo in Hawaii," said the vice president. "Owning property in Kenya would be madness."

Nearby, however, stood a group of one-storey buildings, the centrepiece of which was a hotel — not nearly as modernized as the Golf Hotel, but with running water and electricity. Tatuli, the owner, said that he would not see us out on the street. Pretty dramatic, that. So, on the proverbial back of an envelope, Marie, the ACCES agent, drew plans for an office/house building that Tatuli would build for ACCES. We were delighted.

Before the fourth time that George and I went to Kakamega, I was warned that I would be laying the cornerstone for the great building that was to be called Tsimba House. This assignment sounded as daunting to me as kicking off the ball for the soccer game. I pictured myself, knees bowed, back bent, staggering ten or twenty yards, carrying a huge rock and setting it in the right spot. Would I drop it on my toe? I needn't have worried: this part of the grand ceremony only involved spreading a trowel of cement across an already carefully levelled stone.

In the first years, ACCES agents had no internet contact with Canada, so exchanges of questions and answers, information and advice, were handwritten and sent by regular mail — which seems to us now to be a cumbersome way to do business. As soon as we had a computer in Kakamega, messages were batted back and forth, sometimes almost daily.

Some messages were troublesome. One agent could not abide the water shortage that occurred when the pump in the town broke down. I thought of how Father carried water like a coolie when we lived at the Magritchy place, and I was not as sympathetic as I should have been. A different worry was about a too diligent agent who, having taken it upon herself to inspect and report upon our employees, could find nothing commendable about any of them. Another two women almost never left their apartment for fear of either bugs or men.

We had some trouble with "the constant agent." Kakamega is a great place for a Canadian to spend the winter months. Located very near to the equator, but at 5,000 feet, the climate is almost ideal. What is more, the work of the agent was to give people the help they needed by distributing funds raised in Canada, so Kenyans loved the agents! It was not surprising that there were Canadians who wanted to return to Kenya year after year. We were happy enough to have these experienced people to represent ACCES, but relying upon people who had several turns at the job sometimes proved to be a mistake. Constant agents developed an unhealthy sense of ownership of ACCES so that they did not function as representatives of the board, but as sovereigns of a foreign state. In time we realized that it was better to have this great experience devolve to a number of people, and then to have more and more of them and their friends become converts to ACCES.

We still had another step to take.

After our sixth odyssey to Kakamega, George and I presented to the ACCES board the idea that we should dispense with agents and appoint Kenyans to be in charge of ACCES in their country. We pointed out that Kenyans were capable of managing ACCES overseas just as well as Canadians — indeed, better than Canadians. Kenyans, we said, were more knowledgeable about their country and its needs than we were, and they were intelligent and capable of the leadership and wisdom required for the project's management.

Most members of the board agreed with us and the decision was made to put the Kenyans in charge and trust them to manage the show, with Canadians only standing by. But what a great furor arose then. A number of people, including some of those who had been agents and the most vociferous of whom were the constant agents, were convinced that we would be "robbed blind" and that "ACCES would be down the tube within three years." From some CHES agents and Kenyan bene-factors, we received letters that to us seemed racist. Even our friendly Catholic priest, Father Patrick, said that after thirty years in Kenya he had met no more than one really honest Kenyan. That was the most disappointing message of all.

In hindsight, I believe that the change came about too quickly and that we should have anticipated the opposition that surfaced. But not *that* much opposition. And not that aggressively! It took time before some ACCES supporters were comfortable with the end of our colo-nialist regime, but the ACCES board held steady to its convictions. For the most part our donors held steady too, although there is no doubt that we lost some supporters. In the end we gained more respect than we lost and the ACCES project continued to thrive.

I felt that ACCES had come of age with the end of its paternalistic governance system. We had been following the model we had learned from our predecessor, but now we were confident enough to break free and establish our own international development structure. The end of our colonialism was a measure of the maturity of ACCES.

Literacy for All

Not able to read? Not even able to *read*? Surely learning to read is a basic right of every child. And yet a survey revealed that 10,000 children who lived in the Kakamega district didn't go to school at all. Such a horrible message for an ex-primary teacher to hear. I remembered well the wonder of teaching little children to read and sensing their delight at the magic of "breaking the code" — of making sense of the squiggles on the printed page.

Poverty kept so many children and youth out of school. Fees had to be paid, books purchased, mandatory school uniforms found. The "teacher appreciation fee" was a new development since my teaching days: a box of chocolates at the end of the school year had been appreciation enough for me!

It was more than just the cost of education that kept children away from school. It was also the need for child labour on the *shambas*, the small farms. The heads of families could not part with the help that the young people provided. Although they knew that the way out of poverty was through education, the parents could not manage to grow food for the family if the children were away at school all day. While the mothers carried water and worked on the land, young girls, even six- or seven-year-olds, were needed to mind the babies and the newly ex-babies. The government schools required children to attend from eight in the morning until five in the afternoon. But I had taught young children and knew that they could learn to read with just three or four hours a day. Perhaps they could go to school in the morning and still spend the rest of the day working at home? It was worth a try.

We found that we could use a neighbourhood church for a class-room. As for a teacher, a secondary school graduate could help children learn to read. This plan wasn't immediately successful. We made an unannounced visit to the classroom, only to find the "teacher" reading a book inside and the children running around outside. Wasn't it the children who were supposed to read the book? Many trained teachers were without work, so it was not difficult to find one who was prepared to work for ACCES even for very small wages.

The second major ACCES project, teaching for literacy, was underway.

The new project had barely begun when it started to run away on us. Word of the first class spread rapidly around Kakamega district so that the ACCES office was besieged with elders from other villages petitioning for a school to be provided in their area. Although I was ready to press joyously on, common sense prevailed and we set some limits to the number of schools we would open. ACCES negotiated with the elders: we would supply teachers and a few books if the community could provide a school building, usually a church. We had been in one of these churches with Father Patrick — made of sticks and mud with a dirt floor and one or two small holes for windows. Good enough to begin with. When there were too many children for the original tiny church space, parents quickly busied themselves creating another mud-daub building.

How pleased we were with one another! By the time George and I made our semi-annual trek to Kakamega in 2001, three more literacy classes had begun. We visited each of them, greeted by a great assembly of children and parents. The walls of the mud-daub classrooms would seem to balloon out to enclose us all.

I wondered, could those tiny little children in front of us be old enough to go to school? Surely not. Well, either the parents had pushed them in ahead of time or they were small from lack of nourishment. Probably some of both. On the other hand, at the back of the space stood a few tall boys and girls. Good for them! They were making the best of a chance to be educated and they were not being deterred by classification with much younger children.

"The parents look too old to be mothers and fathers of these children," I commented to a teacher.

"They are too old. You are looking at grandparents. Many of the parents have died of AIDS." Shocking. How horrible to see, right before our eyes, evidence of the sweep of the disease.

But sometimes, rather than being full of grief, my heart almost burst with joy. At one of the parent meetings, a fine looking man stood up to say, "It used to be that, when I had an important letter, I would need to find someone in my village to read it to me. Now my daughter can read it." I shed a tear.

We were thrilled of course by the welcome we received, but amazed also that ACCES had made so much difference to so many people. Wasn't this *saving three lives*?

Superintendent of Schools

Boundaries may have been set, but we still found ourselves in a bind. The parents or guardians were not satisfied that their children would receive only *literacy* education. Would they just learn to read and then be cast adrift? Were they not worthy of the education that other children had?

Now what could we do? How could we say, "Sorry. That's it"? We didn't. We agreed that we would not abandon the pupils after only one or two years in school. We would hire more teachers and teach more grade levels. But where would the funding come from?

We made an interesting discovery: schooling for little children is an easier sell than education for youth who have completed secondary school. Although we kept to our decision to avoid showing photos of runny-nosed little kids covered with flies, we did acquire an arsenal of pictures of smiling children holding tight to a nub of a pencil and a cheap, ruffled scribbler. Now who could deny us a few dollars to help them?

Canadians we knew were also interested in the pictures that showed children drinking from a large mug. We explained that most of the learners would have had no more than a cup of tea — *chai* — before they came to school. By mid-morning the children were dozy. The teachers concluded that the children were lethargic because they were hungry. It was decided that one of the mothers at each school would make a thin porridge called *uji*, using ground maize, the corn that was

Francis Butichi, 2004
Photo by Karen Jensen

grown in the area. Each child would receive a mug of *uji* each day. When possible, the parents or guardians supplied the maize, but during what they called "the hunger season," ACCES paid for it. Each child was required to bring a small stick to build the cooking fire and a bottle of water to mix with the corn meal to make the porridge. For many of these children, that mug of *uji* was their only meal for the whole day. *The hunger season!* How awful.

When attendance of a learner was not regular, it was often because of infections or diseases that could be treated fairly easily — impetigo, ringworm, intestinal worms, jiggers. ACCES arranged to dispatch a nurse-aide to the schools on a regular basis. Even a vitamin pill a day, for a few Canadian pennies, made a noticeable difference to the pupils' health.

Within another two years, the project had grown until it comprised eight schools, a thousand pupils and twenty teachers.

"Now look at this, Beth. Just look at this. A whole damned school district. Now what are we going to do?"

"A school district needs a superintendent, George. What do you think we are going to do? We are going to hire a superintendent." There just happened to be someone waiting in the wings, ready for that very job: Francis Butichi, who had received a CHES and then an ACCES scholarship and now had a bachelor of education degree.

When Francis had not been away at school, he had a habit of hanging around the ACCES office; it was his delight to be allowed to use the computer. So he was right under our feet when we decided to hire an administrator for the primary school project. Francis was diligent, he learned quickly and he served ACCES well. For the community elders and the government officials, he was too young. He had to struggle to be taken seriously by his own people, who venerate age and are suspicious of ambitious youth.

But struggle was not new to Francis. While Francis was still a very small boy, his father abandoned the family. Francis's mother took him and his sisters to live with Grandmother while the mother went to Nairobi to find work. Francis didn't see her again until he was in high school. He never saw his father again.

Mama Uji

Grandmother already had more than enough people to look after. Her two sons, two of her sisters and their four grown children all lived with her in a three-room hut with a thatched roof. Grandmother supported all of them. She had a *shamba*, a half-acre farm, where she grew maize, cassava, arrowroot, yams and potatoes — enough food to keep hunger at bay. And Grandmother used some of her produce to make and sell *chang'aa*, a rough beer, created from part of her maize. She didn't sell all of the beer. She gave everyone in her charge, including the children, enough *chang'aa* that they would fall asleep at night.

In another way, too, Grandmother helped her charges sleep. Even though Kakamega is almost on the equator, it is at 5,000 feet and does become cold at night. So in order to keep them warm, Grandmother traded a bit of her *chang'aa* for a large blanket that she cut into sections. She gave a piece of it to each person in her household. No beds or mattresses — each one slept on a sugar sack on the dirt floor.

The newly acquired little boy, Francis, was a bit of a bother. He was precocious and got in the way of her work. She got tired enough of his audacity that she used some of her precious beer money to send him to school. Not for long, though. As soon as he was big enough, Francis grew and sold *sikuma wiki*, a spinach-like vegetable that is part of the Kenyan diet. That income paid for his school fees until he was out of primary school, and then there were the CHES and ACCES scholarships.

English was Francis's third language. All the same, when he worked for ACCES, the reports he sent to Canada would have made most of us proud to have written them ourselves. Once, when he had sent us a long report on the progress of the ACCES schools, I thanked him and complimented him on his writing. He replied, "It is I who should be thanking you. If it were not for CHES and ACCES, I would be sleeping on a dirt floor with a piece of blanket to cover me."

How pleased we were. An "ACCES graduate" was now employed by ACCES to administer a thriving program that would offer many children a chance at a satisfying life. This is what it was all about. For me, this was the *Something to Do* of happiness.

Tomorrow: Just Here, Yet So Far

After two years, Francis moved on from ACCES. We knew we would not keep him, for he was clever and ambitious. He got a much bigger job managing the education program at a refugee camp in northern Kenya, and later an even bigger job in Darfur with the war-torn refugees of Sudan.

Now what? Where would we find another school superintendent? We felt bereft. But good school administrators did succeed Francis, such as Joseph Mutamba, our current school superintendent.

On our last trip to Kakamega, Joseph asked us to participate at the opening of the ninth primary school. "This opening will be quite different from the others," he warned us, "for many of the people in this area are from the Turkana tribe." Children registered in the other eight schools were almost all Luhya.

Although Joseph told us to expect a different milieu, we were confident that the proceedings would be much as usual. We were wrong.

George and I have been to all of the schools at one time or another — to attend the opening of some and at assemblies of guardians and children at others. We have invariably been wonderfully entertained by the children. I thought about the Christmas concert at Orpha's school so long ago when, on a limping piano, I had accompanied the singing of Canadian children. I thought we carried it off quite well, but "The Teddy Bears' Picnic" would have been utterly eclipsed by the lustiness of the Kenyan choruses.

Quite little children, maybe three years old, will join in with their sisters and brothers, enraptured by the music. Each of the oldest children grabs an empty plastic bottle that has been used to bring water to the school, holds it under one arm and beats out the rhythm with their hands. All of the others sing and all of their bodies move. A particular learner, usually a girl, sings a line of a song that the others echo, then she sings another line that is also echoed and so it goes for a good long time. As we listen to the songs, most often sung in the native Luhya tongue, we will sometimes hear our names. Then we know that the lead girl is honouring us by including us in the words of the song as she goes along. We are charmed.

At the assemblies, we are asked to sit on chairs facing the parents and children, who are perched on rows of long benches in front of us. We stare and smile at one another. The protocol has a standard pattern. On every occasion, a number of officials make speeches, the children entertain us and, as president of ACCES, I am asked to speak.

The opening of School Nine broke the pattern. The formality and etiquette were varied enough to make us just a little uncomfortable and to force a change in our roles.

Guided to sit in the honorary chairs, we looked out at the children massed on one side of the building and the parents and guardians jammed close together on the other side. So far, this was what we had expected. Amongst the adults, we could identify the Turkana — tall, slim people, impressive in their colourful costumes. It was not so impressive, mind you, to see that many of their children looked less healthy than the ones in the other schools that we had visited. Most of the Turkana children looked skinny and many were quite dirty. A waif of maybe six had a baby slung on her back, so that it looked like an extension of her own body. For the first time since we had been visiting the ACCES schools, we were subjected to a fair amount of begging from the Turkana adults. This, we had not expected.

The surprise in the actual proceedings began when, instead of the children dancing and singing, the adults danced for us — a great leaping-in-the-air dance, accompanied by loud singing and guttural grunts. Bending their bodies in deep bows, they almost deposited their heads in our laps as they made an obeisance to each of us as they leapt past. *All of the bows were made to George first.* He was clearly the most honoured guest. I was back-seated again. I whispered to George that this time he would have to make the speech for ACCES.

He did the deed very well, of course. He shouted *ham jambo!* in his loud, ringing voice. *Jambo* means hello, but *ham jambo* means *"Huge hello to all of you!"* The crowd was delighted. They cheered and yelled and stamped their feet and we were almost as excited as they were. Even for a few hours, being immersed in this very different cultural setting increased our awareness of the diversity of the people to whom we could offer help.

Joseph was reflective as we traveled home to Tsimba House. First he wondered if we were offended by the way the Turkana people begged for Kenyan shillings, jostling us around a bit as we left the site. No, no, we assured him. Not at all. Then he mused about the decision to open School Nine. Would it be as successful as the others? Would it thrive? He told us how School Four, called Shitaho, had soared ahead and he asked us to listen to the story of one of the students there.

I have paraphrased that story to keep it close to my heart. Here is Joseph's story.

I went looking for Mercy Mmbone. She is twelve years old. I needed to walk through the Kakamega market, past the noise and the huge crowds — to Masingo slum — to Mercy's home. Mercy lives in a one bedroom shack beside a stagnant ditch that carries sewage. The neighbourhood swarms with cats, dogs, salesmen, drunkards and half-naked children. My greatest surprise comes from these children having fun wading in that sewage ditch, looking for tin cans, old bottles, rusty spoons, bits of metal, maybe some pennies.

Mercy grew up right here, in this ghetto, where she watched drunkards stagger from the *chang'aa* dens, hurling insults at each other and touching small girls freely and carelessly.

This twelve-year-old girl was the last born in a polygamous family of sixteen. To Mercy, her sisters had nothing to show for in their lives, for with no schooling they quickly fell in with the local men and immediately began conceiving one child after another.

Mercy told me how much she wanted to go to school. She said that she couldn't go to the schools that most children in Kakamega attended. Even though her mother did want her to go to school, she could not buy the uniform, pay the desk fee or the teacher appreciation fee, not even a pencil and a book to write in.

But something magical happened: Mercy's mother found out about the ACCES school that was just down the road. At that school, there were no requirements for uniforms or supplies. "I found myself at Shitaho School," Mercy told me, "and that's made me very, very happy."

Not that it was easy for Mercy. The worst part was the way she and the other children at Shitaho were scorned by the ones who attended the state schools. Everyone knew that these Shitaho children were the *very* poor ones in Kakamega, and they were not treated as equals. But more magic happened.

Mercy was allowed to join the pupils at Shitaho who had been trained as a poetry team. These pupils were so passionate and so enjoyed their teamwork that their teacher decided to enter them in a district competitive festival. They were a bit shy about that. Here they were, from a small school, the poorest children in Kakamega, and they were competing with many, many of the government-funded schools in the district. Amazingly, they won! The Shitaho team won!

Mercy could hardly believe it. Now she and her team were entitled to enter the festival for Western Province. Again, they won. They placed first in that competition, too! And you may have guessed — they were entered in the National Festival in Nairobi where they took fourth place. Fourth place in all of Kenya.

Can you imagine such a trip for these children? Can you imagine their excitement and joy? Can you think of the change in the status of that Shitaho School and what a change it made in Mercy's life?

I often tell Joseph's "Mercy Story" to audiences in Canada. Usually, I weep a little and so do they, tears of compassion for people we hardly know.

Lieutenant Governor

George and I have traveled to Kakamega every second year for a total of eight journeys. Our intention is not to impose ourselves upon the Kenyan management of ACCES. The Kenyan people, at least as competent as we are, send their program reports and financial accounts to Canada promptly and efficiently. Indeed, we do not go to Kakamega to help run the show: we go there to keep our passion for ACCES vibrant and to see for ourselves the difference that ACCES is making in the lives of the people there. Aside from the brutally long flights, our visits give us great pleasure.

But sometimes we wonder if we have become "one-note Johnnies." Do we think and talk of nothing but ACCES? Are we social pariahs? We try to maintain some balance, some variety in our activities. One particular series of events took us far from ACCES, adding brilliance to our lives. It came about because of our friendship with Jim Rhodes, who had once been a member of the British Columbia legislature.

Jim and his partner attended banquets in Government House and sometimes he invited us to accompany them. I enjoyed these elegant affairs, taking in the extravagant flower arrangements and staring at the outfits of some of the women. I especially admired the very gracious Lieutenant Governor, the Queen's representative. George found it all a bit of a pain. I admit that the pomp and ceremony could be considered silly — unless you were once a fat little girl from Saskatchewan.

As we dined, I thought about my first formal dinner at the University of Saskatchewan and the errant stuffed olive.

I had a chat with two teenagers who were a part of the British Columbia youth parliament. I talked their ears off about my views on education and then segued into the story of ACCES. Afterwards I felt a bit embarrassed about how much I had yapped away, but George said I was not too outrageous and we both forgot about the episode. But wait.

Two or three weeks later, I received a phone call from one of those young people, who explained that the group was making plans for the youth parliament that would be meeting in the Legislature during the week between Christmas and the New Year. This young man was the youth premier. He asked me to be the Lieutenant Governor. *Lieutenant Governor*! What an honour!

George said, "Well, are you going to do that?"

"What? What? Why on earth would I think of saying no? This is the highlight of my life! I shall represent the Queen! Talk about *Something to Look Forward To*! Of course I am going to do that."

George, of course, got himself right into the spirit of the event. When the day came, he took me to lunch at the impressive Empress Hotel, seating me so that I could look across the road at the tower of the legislative building. I picked at the food on my plate, mucking it around, thinking how unlikely it was for this to be happening.

We were directed to a side door — a *side* door, not the *front* door — and into a musty waiting room that reeked of old glory. The atmosphere was sombre. A Royal Canadian Mounted Police officer, in full scarlet serge, looked bored. I winked at him and he grinned back. The five of us in the cast were herded into a line: the marshall at arms, the kilted piper, the mace bearer, the Lieutenant Governor (me) and, to guard our rear, the RCMP officer. The marshall at arms opened the door of the Legislature and, in the British fashion, yelled a warning to the seated members that the Queen's representative was about to appear. On both sides of the House, the members stood to attention as our solemn group paraded down the red carpet between their ranks, bagpipe blasting. It was a long walk.

The premier had sent very clear instructions about my role: I was to bow to the left, bow to the right, then sit down. I became a white-haired, black-suited rag doll, occupying a much-too-large throne. There was no more than a minute to take in the majestic setting — the red plush, the polished wood — and to locate George in the gallery. Then the performance began.

A page handed me the typed Speech from the Throne, which I read in my clear teacher's voice. Once I had returned the papers to the bearer, the bagpipes skirled again and we made our pompous exit.

I felt a little flat as we made our way home. Was that all there was? Well, not quite. There was a repeat performance when the session was prorogued on New Year's Eve.

This second act ended in disaster. As in Act One, George observed the performance from the gallery. When we had made our solemn exit and he came down the stairs to meet me, he missed the last step and fell. Although he was able to walk, he had hurt his hip badly and was in a frightening amount of pain. We had planned to go to an elegant resort for dinner and New Year's Eve, but we couldn't possibly follow that plan. Instead we drove straight back to our own community and to the hospital emergency room.

We spent New Year's Eve amongst diverse invalids: an elderly gentleman on a stretcher was rushed past all the rest of us; a weeping teenager kept yelling for her mother; a bearded young man cradled his left arm wrapped in a bloody rag. Hours went by. George swore that if we were still there at midnight, he would sing "Auld Lang Syne" in a loud voice. He would have, too. But as we drove home with crutches and medication, he added his voice to those of the revellers that we could hear from the houses along the street.

This was not the celebration we had planned. It was a hard landing after a great flight of fancy. Ah well. It's still fun to remember my role as Lieutenant Governor of British Columbia — icing on the cake of my bonus years.

Elufafwa: A New School

On our eighth visit in Kakamega, we participated in the opening of the newly built Elufafwa School. One of the Canadian Rotary clubs that supports ACCES had provided $17,000 for the construction of this wonderful building. Its opening had been timed for our arrival. A stellar time, this one — an event we shall never forget.

A taxi drove us to the village. As we emerged, we were assaulted by a great chorus of children singing over and over again, "You are welcome, our visitors, you are welcome, *karibu, karibu.*" The throng of children, from wide-eyed little ones to intent older ones, echoed one phrase and then another, led by the strong, strong voice of the student leader. Their song went on and on until we were quite overcome — overcome with joy for only the first time that shining morning.

Once the greetings were finished, the whole crowd of parents, learners and officials walked around the old premises, from the tree stump where the first lessons were taught, to the dark little buildings used as classrooms, where the walls were falling apart, to the little hole of a room for an office. The mud-daub schoolrooms that had been provided by the village elders and that had served the community for seven years were now decaying pitifully. The rooms were so small, so dark, with bumpy dirt floors and with sticks showing through the mud that had been plastered over them to form the walls. The whole place looked abandoned, even though the children had been taught right there until that day.

Now the whole company marched to the new school site. We were meant to enjoy every bit of the day, every bit of the experience, and so all of it was presented in slow, slow motion. The sun beat down on us. I stumbled along the uneven path, less spry than I would have liked.

In the new schoolyard there was a place for everyone to sit. The student desks were arranged outside the pretty L-shaped building, some bleachers were provided for the parents and the teachers. Very fancy seats were arranged for the officials who were honoured with a canopy sheltering us from the burning sun and the rain. (There was some of each before the ceremonies were finished.)

The official party was called on to parade all around the perimeter of the grounds, behind the new school, behind the toilets and all the way to each of the corners, like dogs peeing in the corners to mark their territory. Even the toilets looked new and unused, with four doors for the boys facing front and four for the girls facing back, a modesty wall for the girls still being built even as we passed by. Finishing touches were also being added to the pretty windows of one wing of classrooms.

We shuffled back to our fancy seats. I was distracted by the children, singing and dancing as we traversed the compound, but was assured that there would be much more entertainment before we would leave. Indeed, there was.

How the dancing and singing went on and on! The boys played their plastic water-bucket drums while the girls danced and sang. There were several lead girls who called out their original songs — one dancing almost right in front of us sang, "I shake my body to show my joy."

Speech-making began with a prayer from Pastor One. A plethora of speeches followed — ten in all. Many, many words were discharged into the air around us; too bad they weren't coloured like confetti. Then it was my turn. I asked for a child to stand with me and I was given two of them, so there was one to hold each of my hands as I heaped praise on everyone present. The sun scorched my neck; the rain, only a shower, was just enough to cool us a bit.

For the finale, the whole host followed Pastor One toward the entrance door of the school. The pastor told those of us who were right behind him, "Now we will all walk slowly, slowly, with tiny little steps, just as though we are walking right up to Heaven." And so we did. We walked right up to the door across which there was a wide green ribbon. Pastor Two read a psalm and then, behold, scissors were handed to me to cut the ribbon and a key was given to George to unlock the door. All of the adults rushed into the pristine schoolroom with its wonderful concrete floor, its new brick walls and its pretty windows. There was dancing and jumping and singing and ululating that you could hardly believe.

Magical moments. Moments that fuelled our desire to embrace more and more people within the circle of the ACCES school district.

Secondary School

Now what? The primary schools that we first created as literacy schools were by now complete elementary schools, enrolling 1,300 pupils in all and producing some learners *who had finished standard (grade) eight*. I was speechless when I thought of how the first ACCES schools had begun, with their too-small children and their too-old parents, all trying so valiantly to move out of their grim poverty. But once again we asked ourselves, now what would we do? We had been challenged before about the unfairness of leaving these children behind once they had learned to read, and we had agreed to keep them in school through the primary years. Would we now abandon them when they completed their primary schooling? Not likely. The ACCES board was determined to provide fees and accommodation for our primary school leavers.

The first group comprised nineteen of these students, all of whom ACCES was committed to fund in secondary school. So it was that on our eighth trip to Kakamega, George and I witnessed the next expansion of ACCES: the entry of the nineteen to secondary school.

A supply depot was set up on the grass in front of the ACCES offices at Tsimba House. The students and parents or guardians assembled just as a pickup truck drove in, loaded with mattresses, boxes, blankets, dictionaries, pens, and so on. The secretaries called forth the students one by one to receive the supplies. The whole procedure was organized by the Kenyan office staff, even to details such as the twine and scissors to help the recruits bind their supplies together so that they could be taken home.

George and I went out to shake hands with the parents. Their gratitude was overwhelming. I asked one mother how they would get all of these things home with them and she said, "We just carry them and we are so happy. God bless you." We were the happiest of all.

Soon the whole party left to go into the town to get their uniforms and their shoes.

On the day that our primary school grads enrolled in secondary school, the taxi driver of backing-up-the-hill skill drove us to St. Kizitos Secondary School. We found our students standing in a group near the administration block. They looked a little nervous and were staying close together. I remembered my first days in secondary school, how awkward and insecure I felt. At least these students had uniforms and didn't look different from the other students. In fact, they looked quite wonderful, but how uncomfortable they must have been in the white shirts, the dark green sweaters, the black pants or skirts, the knee socks and the *great stiff shoes*. These children had been used to bare feet, flip-flops or maybe some used runners, and now to be shod in this Oxford-English-style confinement! A recipe for aches and blisters.

We were taken to the principal's office and were greeted with politeness, but not much warmth until it was clearly understood who we were and what kids we had registered. The principal's eyes reflected his pleasure and surprise when he saw the amount on the cheque that Joseph handed to him — a cheque for all of the students for the whole year. This was unusual. Fees were most often paid a little at a time, with many defaults and much chasing home of students.

The principal steered us out to the front gate to have our photos taken with him. He welcomed our kids, told them how lucky they were, and presented a clear admonition about working hard and behaving themselves. We beamed like proud parents. Could these be the same big-eyed barefoot ragamuffins that we had once just hoped to teach to read?

Miraculous!

Celebrating the Years

"No party. I do not want any party. Why would I want to tell everyone that I am seventy years old, have them feel obliged to say the mandatory 'You don't look it at all,' which in fact I do. I don't mind people knowing that I'm seventy, but I can't pretend I'm glad of it and want to celebrate. Celebrate what? Living this long? Looking this old? Wondering if I'll make it to eighty? No party. Please, George, let's think of something else to do."

Poor George. A wife who can't just enjoy food and drink and people, but always has to have something to do. What a harangue. Well, not really "Poor George." George is still not a victim. He was actually really pleased that he didn't have to be involved in some lavish event, or watch me trying to make everything as perfect as I could in the days before, never being satisfied.

Instead, George took me to England to walk in the Dales. What an easy passage through London's Heathrow airport! This was 1998, well before New York was attacked from abroad, before the dreadful bombing in Madrid and the disastrous attack upon the London transportation system. How simple the procedure: no need to remove shoes and belt, or jettison a precious nail file, or watch someone handle the personal items in your carry-on. Our world seemed fairly secure when I was seventy.

A rental car was waiting for us. It seemed to me to have a smirk on its shiny surface, daring us to scratch or dent it. Not my problem: George was the driver. I was the navigator, an assignment I only took on because there was no one else to do it. George was a bold and confident driver; I was a timid and unnatural navigator. I believe that a sense of direction is one of the basic senses, like smell or taste, and that I do not possess that particular sense. It's a pity that I did not inherit it from my father, who possessed an uncanny instinct for direction, as if he had a built-in compass so that he was always able to locate true north. I had been short-changed in the field of navigational intelligence. On my seventieth birthday this deficit sometimes caused a certain testiness from the driver.

We made our way out of London post-haste, scuttling away like country mice. Foreign cities are terrifying for us, especially when we are driving on the wrong side of the road.

Before embarking on the Dales walk, we bumbled along northward, making a detour through part of Scotland. I love the Scottish countryside. George doesn't. Maybe it's masochism that makes me like it — its dour hills, its rather disconsolate villages, its slightly run-down hotels (the ones where we stayed) with their tiny bedrooms and minimal bathrooms, often with street and pub noise from below. And the heather, the heather, the heather.

On to the Dales in Yorkshire — to the quite, quite beautiful hills and valleys. We found our way to small bed-and-breakfast inns from where we could follow paths for short walks across farmers' fields, over stiles and through little villages. From our first journey when he had bought me my gorgeous hat, George had taught me to appreciate out-of-the-way places.

We had planned the charming walks across the farmlands, but we found that it was even more fun to attend unexpected events that we came upon, like the horse auction where scrubby little horses from the moors were being picked up for very little money. There we met a large man of maybe sixty years, dressed in a three-piece tweed suit, looking like a country estate manager. This gent didn't bid on any of the skinny nags; we thought he must be waiting for the presentation of the two huge Clydesdales that we had spied when we arrived. We had to leave when the heavy rain began. Rain also drove us away from a sheep show that we came upon. Pens and pens of sheep — Wensleydale, Lincoln, Leicester, Romney Suffolk, Dorset — all looking wonderfully fat and well-groomed, sporting their great first-prize ribbons. I suppose I was called to these events because of my country roots. On our Saskatchewan farms, we never raised sheep, but we certainly had farm horses. And was I likely to forget the Moose Jaw Fair with all kinds of farm animals sporting colourful ribbons? These English shows warmed my memories.

The trip was *so* much better than a party. Altogether, heralding the new set of years this way was good, gentle fun, appropriate for this time in our lives. Five years later, now seventy-five years old, I said to George, "No party. I do not want any party." Same song. Same response. This time we went to Cornwall for our walking.

Not as good an idea this time, though, for I was quite lame with arthritis in my right foot, the one I had injured badly in that car accident when I was twenty-three. For several years I had been taking an anti-inflammatory medication that had kept me reasonably comfortable. In truth, my mangled foot had hardly bothered me for more than fifty years, yet now all of a sudden it was painful. Well, we had our tickets and how could I tell that the foot wouldn't get better as quickly as it had turned bad? It didn't get better; in fact it got worse. We walked anyway, but my memory of the Land's End of England is of rough beauty and a sore foot.

We cut short our stay in Cornwall, not just because I was lame, but because George was finding it more and more stressful to drive on the wrong side of the road, especially on the narrow, winding trails that we wanted to use to get from one seaside village to another. He swiped off the side mirror on a parked car and, soon after, grazed the left fender on a too-solid fence. I said, "Let's just turn this thing in and get back to London today." So we did.

Upon our return to Canada, a different doctor gave me medication that chastised the arthritis so that walking became a breeze once more. He said, "We must keep you as comfortable as possible for as long as we can." A bit ominous, that. Anyway, I may totter a bit now, but I am still not lame.

After that seventy-fifth birthday, George and I set our minds to work on the business of the sustainability of ACCES. By then the society had clearly made a difference to the lives of many people in

Kenya: a thousand post-secondary students had received scholarships, twelve hundred children were attending the primary schools each year and a few students were in secondary school.

Every time we went to Kakamega, we were more impressed with the difference between the poverty there and the wealth at home. And every time we saw what we could do, we were more convinced that we must rally more people to help the Kenyans.

Since ACCES began, George and I had been in charge of both the leadership and the management of the society. This had to stop. ACCES had grown until its management required the services of a full-time employee, and its leadership had to be assured through a succession of qualified presidents and vice presidents. So George and I resigned from our positions. With us no longer hard-wired as the leaders, others stepped in, adding knowledge, skill and creativity to the organization. Now ACCES had the capacity for continuity and could be sustained long after George and I were out of the picture.

We experienced some trauma as we loosened our hold upon ACCES. I did not readily accept the fact that I was not the first to know about every accomplishment, every stir or stumble. It was not easy to relegate ourselves to the back seat, especially for me with my back seat phobia, and to let others navigate and drive ACCES. But that has been done.

Well-qualified executive members for the positions of vice president and then president were right before our eyes — people who had held leadership positions in their work life and were now retired and ready for further challenge just as George and I had been. Nor was it difficult to hire an executive director. Little by little our leadership and management duties became the responsibility of other people and the progress of ACCES was sustained. Eventually, the office was moved out of our home and into a space in downtown Vancouver.

Now our email, posted mail and telephone calls are reduced to a tenth of what they were not so long ago. We are both active on the ACCES board and we still entertain and make speeches for the society, but ACCES is no longer primarily our responsibility. Our *Something to Do* has been trimmed to fit our level of energy.

Happiness After All

Now that I am in my eightieth year, what do I have to say about this matter of happiness? I have told my friends that the past fifteen years have been the happiest years of my life. Can this be true? Have these years affirmed the validity of the happiness formula?

It is fair to say that the *Someone to Love* element of the formula is being whittled away until there are no longer aunts and uncles, nor even Mother and Father. In fact, there is no longer a generation older than our own. Now that is a perilous thought. And in our own generation, detailing each person's medical report — joints, blood pressure, hearing — is the first item in most conversations. The only good that seems to accrue from that is the increased appreciation that we feel for those who are still part of our lives. Most valued is the love that George and I have for one another.

Although we have been losing old friends during the past fifteen years, we have acquired many new ones. I think George and I have been unusually lucky, for we are in a position to make new friends because of ACCES. We are also constantly reminded of the mutual delight we find in each other and the exciting work that we do together.

So, in our senior years, we are still surrounded by people to love and people who love us. The *Someone to Love* has become the *Many Ones to Love*.

The last time I wrote about the happiness formula, I suggested that the *Something to Do* was not satisfying unless whatever was being done resulted in an accomplishment or an achievement. Now I have learned an additional quality that enhances this element: what is being done should have a clear purpose. George and I have often been praised for our work as the founders of ACCES. We always reply that we are the ones that have received the greatest rewards. That is not modesty; it is the truth. ACCES has given us *Something to Do* that has a purpose and that purpose brings us joy.

As I watch other retired people, I have noticed that there appear to be certain post-retirement stages. In Stage One, there is energy and a will to continue to work at a project or toward a goal; after a time, in Stage Two, taking care of the essential tasks of home, food, family and health are all-consuming; finally, in Stage Three, people need to be cared for. In all three stages, including the last one, life can have a purpose. It behooves us to stay in Stage One for as long as possible with a dominant objective, perhaps waning as age depletes energy but still with an external goal in focus. In the second stage, retirement from outside activities may be necessary, but pride of independence and a cheerful attitude are worthy objectives. And in the final stage, we can try to live out our lives with dignity and grace. We can always have the *Something to Do.*

The *Something to Look Forward To* has become increasingly important for us, but at the same time, increasingly easy to find. In order to postpone our collapse into life in our own particular armchairs, we set goals — but ones that are easy enough to reach with our reduced energy. There are short-term objectives, like planting more perennials than annuals in our garden, and more ambitious, longer-term plans, such as going to Kenya again next year. All three elements of happiness have been qualified with experience and with the aging process.

I say to George, "Pinch me. Just pinch me so I can be sure that I am not dreaming. Can this life of ours be real? How did this fat little girl from Saskatchewan find such happiness? Can I really have all of this: *Someone to Love, Something to Do,* and *Something to Look Forward To?*" Pinch me.

INDEX

ACCES

The African Canadian Continuing Education Society (ACCES), a non-profit society with charitable status, was founded by George and Beth Scott in 1993. The mission of ACCES is to help young Africans obtain the skills and education needed to benefit themselves and their society.

The ACCES Foundation was formed in 1997 to provide long term support for ACCES. Donations to the ACCES Foundation are wisely invested, with the accrued funds used for the Society's programs. The ACCES Foundation also has charitable status.

Since their inception, ACCES and the ACCES Foundation have provided

- ten primary schools for over 1,200 Kenyan children, including AIDS orphans, who could not otherwise afford to learn to read and write
- secondary education for the graduates of these primary schools
- post-secondary scholarships for more than 1,200 Kenyans to study in Kenya
- HIV/AIDS education for thousands of teachers and community members
- business training and micro-credit for hundreds of small-business entrepreneurs.

All donations designated for ACCES programs are used for that purpose. Administrative costs are funded by other specified donations.

Net proceeds from the sale of *Pinch Me* will be donated to ACCES.

AFRICAN
CANADIAN
CONTINUING
EDUCATION
SOCIETY

Contact:
ACCES
#402 – 411 Dunsmuir St.
Vancouver, BC   V6B 1X4
(604) 688-4880
info@acceskenya.org
www.acceskenya.org

Beth Rowles Scott grew up in rural Saskatchewan in the 1930s and completed a teacher's certificate at the University of Saskatchewan, assuming teaching positions in Big River and Saskatoon. After moving to British Columbia, she took up teaching and administration positions in the Surrey school district, where she later became a secondary school principal, the only female secondary principal in BC at the time. After her retirement, Beth obtained her doctorate in educational administration from the University of British Columbia.

Beth and her husband, George Scott, are the founders of the African Canadian Continuing Education Society (ACCES). The organization has provided education funding and facilities for thousands of children and young adults in rural Kenya. In 2006, the Scotts were recognized as "Outstanding Canadians" by the Corporation of the City of White Rock, BC, and Beth was named "Woman of the Year" by Soroptomist International of White Rock, an organization devoted to improving the lives of women and girls in the community and the world.

The Scotts live on a bluff overlooking Crescent Beach in Surrey, British Columbia. Beth is currently writing a novel, a tale of dramatic events centred on a troubled First Nations reserve.